A Treasury of Christmas Stories

A Treasury of Christmas Stories

Henry Van Dyke

edited by James S. Bell, Jr.

Harold Shaw Publishers
Wheaton, Illinois

ISBN 0-87788-817-5

Cover design and illustrations © 1993 by David LaPlaca

Library of Congress Cataloging-in-Publication Data

Van Dyke, Henry, 1852-1933.
A Treasury of Christmas Stories / Henry Van Dyke : James S. Bell, Jr., editor.
   p.   cm.
  ISBN 0-87788-817-5
  1. Christmas—Literary collections.   I. Bell, James S., Jr.
II. Title.
PS3117.T74 1993
813'.52—dc20   92-46869
                          CIP

---

99 98 97 96 95 94

10 9 8 7 6 5 4 3 2

To Peter Shearn, connoisseur of the entire Van Dyke corpus;
in remembrance of Bryant Pond, Maine, 1985,
when you first introduced me to H.V.D.

· Good books build good friendships.

Contents

Introduction

For some of us, reading is a required tradition during the Christmas season. I don't mean ordinary books that we catch up on during the holiday vacation. Rather, we long for an ambience that evokes that timeless sense of magic and holiness that is often called "the spirit of Christmas." Of course we need to reread the nativity story to savor its pure essence. Yet we hunger for more. With nearly two thousand Christmases behind us, nostalgia must be satiated. My fixation on the spirit of Christmas past takes the form of reading the George MacDonald Christmas stories to my children and entering the quaint world of the English country squire in the early 1800s found in Washington Irving's *Sketchbook of Geoffrey Crayon.*

Yet where is that elusive volume of stories that creatively expands on the nativity theme as well as other spiritual and historical dimensions of the Yuletide? Enter Henry Van Dyke! His short story parable "The Other Wise Man" seems to survive staying in print and is becoming a classic of sorts.

What the contemporary reader is not aware of is that Van Dyke was a prolific and eclectic writer of theology, short stories, poems, outdoor life, literary studies, and so on. The real discovery, for the Christmas reader, however, is that Van Dyke had a love affair with every aspect of the church feast. As an evangelical believer, he called Christmas the "sunrise of the Bible" and made it either a central theme or a backdrop to numerous short stories, devotions, poems, and prayers. It is from this plethora of material that I have compiled this treasury.

The Reverend Henry Van Dyke (1852-1933) was a poet, essayist, and short-story writer, as well as a Murray Professor of English at Princeton University. In conjunction with his literary avocation, Van Dyke's true calling was to communicate the gospel. He was an evangelical Presbyterian who was one of America's most renowned preachers at Brick Church in New York City, where his sermons became famous. He was a prominent defender of orthodoxy on denominational committees, an author of books on theology, a hymn writer, and active at Princeton Theological Seminary. In this respect he was remembered for *The Gospel in an Age of Doubt*. Perhaps one of the most notable achievements of his career was his appointment by Woodrow Wilson as minister to the Netherlands and Luxembourg in 1913.

Van Dyke was also a keen fisherman, spending much time in the Canadian wilds. His son wrote, "To him romance was never distance; it was rather the vital quality of being alive among men and amid the unfathomable wonders of nature." I have detected in the stories contained herein a taste of the mystical vision of nature found in the mythic works of George MacDonald, a contemporary of his. Indeed, both were enamored with the romantic poetry of the German writer Novalis. MacDonald translated this work, and Van Dyke named his most noted book of short stories, *The Blue Flower*, after Novalis' work. C. S. Lewis also spoke of *The Blue Flower* in relation to romantic longing, or desire for the Wholly Other.

What qualities make his Christmas stories appealing? The nativity event, though written in a straightforward manner, is pregnant with joy, mystery, and wonder. We long for a more expansive version with different perspectives and greater detail. The author employs the fictional short story to speculate on other aspects of the birth of our Lord, creating characters who grow in new ways as a result of their encounter with this awesome occasion.

"The Other Wise Man," "Even unto Bethlehem," and "The Sad Shepherd" fall into this category. "The Christmas Angel" is similar, except that we view this grand event from the ethereal halls of heaven. Angels engaged in a type of dialectic over man's sin cannot anticipate the unique solution of the Incarnation—until it's announced by this little angel.

Van Dyke excels in his descriptive abilities, especially of nature. He wrote his own volume on the Holy Land, and this authenticity saturates the aforementioned nativity stories. He is at home in the fourth-century Antioch of "The Lost Word" and the sixth century of St. Boniface and the German heathen of "The First Christmas Tree." He imbues these two stories with almost a folk-tale, dreamlike quality that satisfies our need for not only the nostalgic, but the slightly exotic or even esoteric as well. I especially like the scents, sounds, and scenery of the deep snow-filled German woods as Boniface carries his cross by sled to a future pagan sacrifice at Christmas.

One can sense traces of many influences upon reading this volume—Classic, Romantic, Biblical, plus the impact of his late Victorian culture. For the sake of diversity and inspiration I've also sprinkled throughout bits of sermons, devotions, poems, and prayers that further exalt the significance of the birth of the Savior.

My fond hope is that you will dip into this volume each Christmas for inspiration and to escape (for a time) the ambience of mere shopping malls. *A Treasury of Christmas Stories* will hopefully rejuvenate that childlike joy of past special times and places and add to their rich meaning. This spirit of Christmas we speak of is, after all, the pervasive Spirit of Christ. In the words of Van Dyke himself, there is a better thing than merely observing Christmas day, and that is keeping Christmas:

> *Are you willing to believe that . . . the*
> *blessed life which began in Bethlehem*
> *nineteen hundred years ago is the image*
> *and brightness of the Eternal Love?*
> *Then you can keep Christmas. And if*
> *you keep it for a day, why not always?*
> *But you can never keep it alone.*

James S. Bell, Jr.

The Other Wise Man

ou know the story of the Three Wise Men of the East, and how they travelled from far away to offer their gifts at the manger-cradle in Bethlehem. But have you ever heard the story of the Other Wise Man, who also saw the star in its rising, and set out to follow it, yet did not arrive with his brethren in the presence of the young child Jesus? Of the great desire of this fourth pilgrim, and how it was denied, yet accomplished in the denial; of his many wanderings and testings of his soul; of the long way of his seeking and the strange way of his finding the One whom he sought—I would tell the tale as I have heard fragments of it in the Hall of Dreams, in the palace of the Heart of Man.

In the days when Augustus Caesar was master of many kings and Herod reigned in Jerusalem, there lived in the city of Ecbatana, among the mountains of Persia, a certain man named Artaban. His house stood close to the outermost of the walls which encircled the royal treasury. From his roof he could look over the seven-fold battlements of black and white and crimson and blue and red and silver and gold, to the hill where the summer palace of the Parthian emperors glittered like a jewel in a crown.

Around the dwelling of Artaban spread a fair garden, a tangle of flowers and fruit-trees, watered by a score of streams descending from the slopes of Mount Orontes, and made musical by innumerable birds. But all colour was lost in the soft and odorous darkness of the late September night, and all sounds were hushed in the deep charm of its silence, save the splashing of the water, like a voice half-sobbing and half-laughing under the shadows. High above the trees a dim glow of light shone through the curtained arches of the upper chamber, where the master of the house was holding council with his friends.

He stood by the doorway to greet his guests—a tall, dark man of about forty years, with brilliant eyes set near together under his broad brow, and firm lines graven around his fine, thin lips; the brow of a dreamer and the mouth of a soldier, a man of sensitive feelings but inflexible will—one of those who, in whatever age they may live, are born for inward conflict and a life of quest.

His robe was of pure white wool, thrown over a tunic of silk; and a white, pointed cap, with long lapels at the sides, rested on his flowing black hair. It was the dress of the ancient priesthood of the Magi, called the fire-worshippers.

"Welcome!" he said, in his low, pleasant voice, as one after another entered the room—"Welcome, Abdus; peace be with you, Rhodaspes and Tigranes, and with you my father, Abgarus. You are all welcome. This house grows bright with the joy of your presence."

There were nine of the men, differing widely in age, but alike in the richness of their dress of many-coloured silks, and in the massive golden collars around their necks, marking them as Parthian nobles, and in the winged circles of gold resting upon their breasts, the sign of followers of Zoroaster.

They took their places around a small black altar at the end of the room, where a tiny flame was burning. Artaban, standing beside it, and waving a barsom of thin tamarisk branches above the fire, fed it with dry sticks of pine and fragrant oils. Then he began the ancient chant of the Yasna, and the voices of his companions joined in the hymn to Ahura-Mazda:

> We worship the Spirit Divine,
>> all wisdom and goodness possessing,
> Surrounded by Holy Immortals,
>> the givers of bounty and blessing;
> We joy in the work of His hands,
>> His truth and His power confessing.

> We praise all the things that are pure,
>> for these are His only Creation;
> The thoughts that are true, and the words
>> and the deeds that have won approbation;
> These are supported by Him,
>> and for these we make adoration.

> Hear us, O Mazda! Thou livest
>> in truth and in heavenly gladness;
> Cleanse us from falsehood, and keep us
>> from evil and bondage to badness;
> Pour out the light and the joy of Thy life
>> on our darkness and sadness.

> Shine on our gardens and fields,
>> shine on our working and weaving;

Shine on the whole race of man,
                   believing and unbelieving;
Shine on us now through the night,
Shine on us now in Thy might,
The flame of our holy love
                and the song of our worship receiving.

The fire rose with the chant, throbbing as if the flame responded to the music, until it cast a bright illumination through the whole apartment, revealing its simplicity and splendour.

The floor was laid with tiles of dark blue veined with white; columns of twisted silver stood out against the blue walls; the clear-story of round-arched windows above them was hung with azure silk; the vaulted ceiling was a pavement of blue stones, like the body of heaven in its clearness, sown with silver stars. From the four corners of the roof hung four golden magic-wheels, called the tongues of the gods. At the eastern end, behind the altar, there were two dark-red pillars of porphyry; above them a lintel of the same stone, on which was carved the figure of a winged archer, with his arrow set to the string and his bow drawn.

The doorway between the pillars, which opened upon the terrace of the roof, was covered with a heavy curtain of the colour of a ripe pomegranate, embroidered with innumerable golden rays shooting upward from the floor. In effect the room was like a quiet, starry night, all azure and silver, flushed in the east with the rosy promise of the dawn. It was, as the house of a man should be, an expression of the character and spirit of the master.

He turned to his friends when the song was ended, and invited them to be seated on the divan at the western end of the room.

"You have come to-night," said he, looking around the circle, "at my call, as the faithful scholars of Zoroaster, to renew your worship and rekindle your faith in the God of Purity, even as this fire has been rekindled on the altar. We worship not the fire, but Him of whom it is the chosen symbol, because it is the purest of all created things. It speaks to us of one who is Light and Truth. Is it not so, my father?"

"It is well said, my son," answered the venerable Abgarus. "The enlightened are never idolaters. They lift the veil of form and go in the shrine of reality, and new light and truth are coming to them continually through the old symbols."

"Hear me then, my father and my friends," said Artaban, "while I tell you of the new light and truth that have come to me through the most ancient of all signs. We have searched the secrets of Nature together, and studied the healing virtues of water and fire and the plants. We have read also the books of prophecy in which the future is dimly foretold in words that are hard to understand. But the highest of all learning is the knowledge of the stars. To trace their course is to untangle the threads of the mystery of life from the beginning to the end. If we could follow them perfectly, nothing would be hidden from us. But is not our knowledge of them still incomplete? Are there not many stars still beyond our horizon—lights that are known only to the dwellers in the far south-land, among the spice-trees of Punt and the gold mines of Ophir?"

There was a murmur of assent among the listeners.

"The stars," said Tigranes, "are the thoughts of the Eternal. They are numberless. But the thoughts of man can be counted, like the years of his life. The wisdom of the Magi is the greatest of all wisdoms on earth, because it knows its own ignorance. And that is the secret of power. We keep men always looking and waiting for a new sunrise. But we ourselves understand that the darkness is equal to the light, and that the conflict between them will never be ended."

"That does not satisfy me," answered Artaban, "for, if the waiting must be endless, if there could be no fulfillment of it, then it would not be wisdom to look and wait. We should become like those new teachers of the Greeks, who say that there is no truth, and that the only wise men are those who spend their lives in discovering and exposing the lies that have been believed in the world. But the new sunrise will certainly appear in the appointed time. Do not our own books tell us that this will come to pass, and that men will see the brightness of a great light?"

"That is true," said the voice of Abgarus. "Every faithful disciple of Zoroaster knows the prophecy of the Avesta, and carries the word in his heart. 'In that day Sosiosh the Victorious shall arise out of the number of the prophets in the east country. Around him shall shine a mighty brightness, and he shall make life everlasting, incorruptible, and immortal, and the dead shall rise again.'"

"This is a dark saying," said Tigranes, "and it may be that we shall never understand it. It is better to consider the things that are near at hand, and to increase the influence of the Magi in their own country, rather than to look for one who may be a stranger, and to whom we must resign our power."

The others seemed to approve these words. There was a silent feeling of agreement manifest among them; their looks responded with that indefinable expression which always follows when a speaker has uttered the thought that has been slumbering in the hearts of his listeners. But Artaban turned to Abgarus with a glow on his face, and said:

"My father, I have kept this prophecy in the secret place of my soul. Religion without a great hope would be like an altar without a living fire. And now the flame has burned more brightly, and by the light of it I have read other words which also have come from the fountain of

Truth, and speak yet more clearly of the rising of the Victorious One in his brightness."

He drew from the breast of his tunic two small rolls of fine parchment, with writing upon them, and unfolded them carefully upon his knee.

"In the years that are lost in the past, long before our fathers came into the land of Babylon, there were wise men in Chaldea, from whom the first of the Magi learned the secret of the heavens. And of these Balaam the son of Beor was one of the mightiest. Hear the words of his prophecy: 'There shall come a star out of Jacob, and a scepter shall arise out of Israel.' "

The lips of Tigranes drew downward with contempt, as he said, "Judah was a captive by the waters of Babylon, and the sons of Jacob were in bondage to our kings. The tribes of Israel are scattered through the mountains like lost sheep, and from the remnant that swells in Judea under the yoke of Rome neither star nor scepter shall arise."

"And yet," answered Artaban, "it was the Hebrew Daniel, the mighty searcher of dreams, the counsellor of kings, the wise Belteshazzar, who was most honoured and beloved of our great King Cyrus. A prophet of sure things and a reader of the thoughts of the Eternal, Daniel proved himself to our people. And these are the words that he wrote." (Artaban read from the second roll.) " 'Know, therefore, and understand that from the going forth of the commandment to restore Jerusalem, unto the Anointed One, the Prince, the time shall be seven and threescore and two weeks.'"

"But, my son," said Abgarus, doubtfully, "these are mystical numbers. Who can interpret them, or who can find the key that shall unlock their meaning?"

Artaban answered, "It has been shown to me and to my three companions among the Magi—Caspar, Melchior, and Balthazar. We have searched the ancient tablets of Chaldea and computed the time. It falls in this year. We have studied the sky, and in the spring of the year we saw two of the greatest planets draw near together in the sign of the Fish, which is the house of the Hebrews. We also saw a new star there, which shone for one night and then vanished. Now again the two great planets are meeting. This night is their conjunction. My three brothers are watching by the ancient Temple of the Seven Spheres, at Borsippa, in Babylonia, and I am watching here. If the star shines again, they will wait ten days for me at the temple, and then we will set out together for Jerusalem, to see and worship the promised one who shall be born King of Israel. I believe the sign will come. I have made ready for the journey. I have sold my possessions, and bought these three jewels—a sapphire, a ruby, and a pearl—to carry them as tribute to the King. And I ask you to go with me on the pilgrimage, that we may have joy together in finding the Prince who is worthy to be served."

While he was speaking he thrust his hand into the inmost fold of his girdle and drew out three great gems—one blue as a fragment of the night sky, one redder than a ray of sunrise, and one as pure as the peak of a snow-mountain at twilight—and laid them on the outspread scrolls before him.

But his friends looked on with strange and alien eyes. A veil of doubt and mistrust came over their faces, like a fog creeping up from the marshes to hide the hills. They glanced at each other with looks of wonder and pity, as those who have listened to incredible sayings, the story of a wild vision, or the proposal of an impossible enterprise.

At last Tigranes said, "Artaban, this is a vain dream. It comes from too much looking upon the stars and the cherishing of lofty thoughts. It would be wiser to spend the time in gathering money for the new fire-temple at Chala. No king will ever rise from the broken race of Israel, and no end will ever come to the eternal strife of light and darkness. He who looks for it is a chaser of shadows. Farewell."

And another one said, "Artaban, I have no knowledge of these things, and my office as guardian of the royal treasure binds me here. The quest is not for me. But if thou must follow it, fare thee well."

And another said, "In my house there sleeps a new bride, and I cannot leave her nor take her with me on this strange journey. This quest is not for me. But may thy steps be prospered wherever thou goest. So, farewell."

And another said, "I am ill and unfit for hardship, but there is a man among my servants whom I will send with thee when thou goest, to bring me word how thou farest."

So, one by one, they left the house of Artaban. But Abgarus, the oldest and the one who loved him the best, lingered after the others had gone, and said, gravely, "My son, it may be that the light of truth is in this sign that has appeared in the skies, and then it will surely lead to the Prince and the mighty brightness. Or it may be that it is only a shadow of the light, as Tigranes has said, and then he who follows it will have a long pilgrimage and a fruitless search. But it is better to follow even the shadow of the best than to remain content with the worst. And those who would see wonderful things must often be ready to travel alone. I am too old for this journey, but my heart shall be a companion of thy pilgrimage day and night, and I shall know the end of thy quest. Go in peace."

Then Abgarus went out of the azure chamber with its silver stars, and Artaban was left in solitude.

He gathered up the jewels and replaced them in his girdle. For a long time he stood and watched the flame that flickered and sank upon the altar. Then he crossed the hall, lifted the heavy curtain, and passed out between the pillars of porphyry to the terrace on the roof.

The shiver that runs through the earth ere she rouses from her night-sleep had already begun, and the cool wind that heralds the daybreak was drawing downward from the lofty snow-traced ravines of Mount Orontes. Birds, half-awakened, crept and chirped among the rustling leaves, and the smell of ripened grapes came in brief wafts from the arbors.

Far over the eastern plain a white mist stretched like a lake. But where the distant peaks of Zagros cut into the western horizon the sky was clear. Jupiter and Saturn rolled together like drops of flame about to blend in one.

As Artaban watched them, a steel-blue spark was born out of the darkness beneath, rounding itself with purple splendours to a crimson sphere, and springing upward through rays of saffron and orange into a point of white radiance. Tiny and infinitely remote, yet perfect in every part, it pulsated in the enormous vault as if the three jewels in the Magian's girdle had mingled and been transformed into a living heart of light.

He bowed his head. He covered his brow with his hands.

"It is the sign," he said. "The King is coming, and I will go to meet him."

All night long, Vasda, the swiftest of Artaban's horses, had been waiting, saddled and bridled, in her stall, pawing the ground impatiently, and shaking her bit as if she shared the eagerness of her master's purpose, though she knew not its meaning.

Before the birds had fully roused to their strong, high, joyful chant of morning song, before the white mist had begun to lift lazily from the plain, the Other Wise Man was in the saddle, riding swiftly along the high-road, which skirted the base of Mount Orontes, westward.

How close, how intimate is the comradeship between a man and his favorite horse on a long journey. It is a silent, comprehensive friendship, an intercourse beyond the need of words.

They drink at the same way-side springs, and sleep under the same guardian stars. They are conscious together of the subduing spell of nightfall and the quickening joy of daybreak. The master shares his evening meal with his hungry companion, and feels the soft, moist lips caressing the palm of his hand as they close over the morsel of bread. In the gray dawn he is roused from his encampment by the gentle stir of a warm, sweet breath over his sleeping face, and looks up into the eyes of his faithful fellow-traveller, ready and waiting for the toil of the day. Surely, unless he is a pagan and an unbeliever, by whatever name he calls upon his God, he will thank Him for this voiceless sympathy, this quiet affection, and his morning prayer will embrace a double blessing—God bless us both, the horse and the rider, and keep our feet from falling and our souls from death!

Then, through the keen morning air, the swift hoofs beat their tattoo along the road, keeping time to the pulsing of two hearts that are moved with the same eager desire—to conquer space, to devour the distance, to attain the goal of the journey.

Artaban must indeed ride wisely and well if he would keep the appointed hour with the other Magi; for the route was about five hundred miles, and fifteen was the utmost that he could travel in a day. But he knew Vasda's strength, and pushed forward without anxiety, making the fixed distance every day, though he must travel late into the night, and in the morning long before sunrise.

He passed along the brown slopes of Mount Orontes, furrowed by the rocky courses of a hundred torrents.

He crossed the level plains of the Nisaeans, where the famous herds of horses, feeding in the wide pastures, tossed their heads at Vasda's approach, and galloped away with a thunder of many hoofs, and flocks of wild birds rose suddenly from the swampy meadows, wheeling in great circles with a shining flutter of innumerable wings and shrill cries of surprise.

He traversed the fertile fields of Concabar, where the dust from the threshing-floors filled the air with a golden mist, half hiding the huge temple of Astarte with its four hundred pillars.

At Baghistan, among the rich gardens watered by fountains from the rock, he looked up at the mountain thrusting its immense rugged brow out over the road, and saw the figure of King Darius trampling upon his fallen foes, and the proud list of his wars and conquests graven high upon the face of the eternal cliff.

Over many a cold and desolate pass, crawling painfully across the wind-swept shoulders of the hills; down many a black mountain-gorge, where the river roared and raced before him like a savage guide; across many a smiling vale, with terraces of yellow limestone full of vines and fruit-trees; through the oak-groves of Carine and the dark Gates for Zagros, walled in by precipices; into the ancient city of Chawla, where the people of Samaria had been kept in captivity long ago; and out again by the mighty portal, cut through the encircling hills, where he saw the image of the High Priest of the Magi sculptured in the wall of rock, with hand uplifted as if to bless the centuries of pilgrims; past the entrance of the narrow mountain passage, filled from end to end with orchards of peaches and figs, through which the river Gyndes foamed down to meet him; over the broad rice-fields, where the autumnal vapours spread their deathly mists; following along the course of the river, under tremulous shadows of poplar and tamarind, among the lower hills; and out upon the flat plain, where the road ran straight as an arrow through the stubble-fields and parched meadows; past the city of Ctesiphon, where the Parthian emperors reigned, and the vast metropolis of Seleucia which Alexander built; across the swirling floods of Tigris and the many channels of Euphrates, flowing yellow through the corn-lands—Artaban pressed onward until he arrived, at nightfall on the tenth day, beneath the shattered walls of populous Babylon.

Vasda was almost spent, and Artaban would gladly have turned into the city to find rest and refreshment for himself and for her. But he knew that it was three hours journey yet to the Temple of the Seven Spheres, and he must reach the place by midnight if he would find his comrades waiting. So he did not halt, but rode steadily across the stubble-fields.

A grove of date palms made an island of gloom in the pale yellow sea. As she passed into the shadow, Vasda slackened her pace, and began to pick her way more carefully.

Near the farther end of the darkness an access of caution seemed to fall upon her. She scented some danger of difficulty; it was not in her heart to fly from it—only to be prepared for it, and to meet it wisely, as a good horse should do. The grove was close and silent as the tomb; not a leaf rustled, not a bird sang.

She felt her steps before her delicately, carrying her head low, and sighing now and then with apprehension. At last she gave a quick breath of anxiety and dismay, and stood stock-still, quivering in every muscle, before a dark object in the shadow of the last palm-tree.

Artaban dismounted. The dim starlight revealed the form of a man lying across the road. His humble dress and the outline of his haggard face showed that he was probably one of the Hebrews who still dwelt in great numbers around the city. His pallid skin, dry and yellow as parchment, bore the mark of the deadly fever which ravaged the marsh-lands in autumn. The chill of death was in his lean hand, and, as Artaban released it, the arm fell back inertly upon the motionless breast.

He turned away with a thought of pity, leaving the body to that strange burial which the Magians deemed most fitting—the funeral of the desert, from which the kites and vultures rise on dark wings, and the beasts of prey slink furtively away. When they are gone there is only a heap of white bones on the sand.

But, as he turned, a long, faint, ghostly sigh came from the man's lips. The bony fingers gripped the hem of the Magian's robe and held him fast.

Artaban's heart leaped to his throat, not with fear, but with a speechless resentment at the importunity of this blind delay.

How could he stay here in the darkness to minister to a dying stranger? What claim had this unknown fragment of human life upon his compassion or his service? If he lingered but for an hour he could hardly reach Borsippa at the appointed time. His companions would think he had given up the journey. They would go without him. He would lose his quest.

But if he went on now, the man would surely die. If Artaban stayed, life might be restored. His spirit throbbed and fluttered with the urgency of the crisis. Should he risk the great reward of his faith for the sake of a single deed of charity? Should he turn aside, if only for a moment from the following of the star, to give a cup of cold water to a poor, perishing Hebrew?

"God of truth and purity," he prayed, "direct me in the holy path, the way of wisdom which Thou only knowest."

Then he turned back to the sick man. Loosening the grasp of his hand, he carried him to a little mound at the foot of the palm-tree.

He unbound the thick folds to the turban and opened the garment above the sunken breast. He brought water from one of the small canals near by, and moistened the sufferer's brow and mouth. He mingled a draught of one of those simple but potent remedies which he carried always in his girdle—for the Magians were physicians as well as astrologers—and poured it slowly between the colourless lips. Hour after hour he laboured as only a skillful healer of disease can do. At last the man's strength returned; he sat up and looked about him.

"Who art thou?" he said, in the rude dialect of the country, "and why hast thou sought me here to bring back my life?"

"I am Artaban the Magian, of the city of Ecbatana, and I am going to Jerusalem in search of one who is to be born King of the Jews, a great Prince and Deliverer of all men. I dare not delay any longer upon my journey, for the caravan that has waited for me may depart without me. But see, here is all that I have left of bread and wine, and here is a potion of healing herbs. When thy strength is restored thou canst find the dwellings of the Hebrews among the houses of Babylon."

The Jew raised his trembling hand solemnly to heaven.

"Now may the God of Abraham and Isaac and Jacob bless and prosper the journey of the merciful, and bring him in peace to his desired haven. Stay! I have nothing to give thee in return—only this: that I can tell thee where the Messiah must be sought. For our prophets have said that he should be born not in Jerusalem, but in Bethlehem of Judah. May the Lord bring thee in safety to that place, because thou hast had pity upon the sick."

It was already long past midnight. Artaban rode in haste, and Vasda, restored by the brief rest, ran eagerly through the silent plain and swam the channels of the river. She put forth the remnant of her strength, and fled over the ground like a gazelle.

But the first beam of the rising sun set a long shadow before her as she entered upon the final track of the journey, and the eyes of Artaban, anxiously scanning the great mound of Nimrod and the Temple of the Seven Spheres, could discern no trace of his friends.

The many-coloured terraces of black and orange and red and

yellow and green and blue and white, shattered by the convulsions of nature, and crumbling under the repeated blows of human violence, still glittered like a ruined rainbow in the morning light.

Artaban rode swiftly around the hill. He dismounted and climbed to the highest terrace, looking out toward the west.

The huge desolation of the marshes stretched away to the horizon and the border of the desert. Herons stood by the stagnant pools and jackals skulked through the low bushes; but there was no sign of the caravan of the Wise Men, far or near.

At the edge of the terrace he saw a little cairn of broken bricks, and under them a piece of papyrus. He caught it up and read: "We have waited past the midnight, and can delay no longer. We go to find the King. Follow us across the desert."

Artaban sat down upon the ground and covered his head in despair.

"How can I cross the desert," said he, "with no food and a spent horse? I must return to Babylon, sell my sapphire, and buy a train of camels, and provisions for the journey. I may never overtake my friends. Only God the merciful knows whether I shall not lose sight of the King because I tarried to show mercy."

There was a silence in the Hall of Dreams, where I was listening to the story of the Other Wise Man. Through the silence I saw, but very dimly, his figure passing over the dreary undulations of the desert, high upon the back of his camel, rocking steadily onward like a ship over the waves.

The land of death spread its cruel net around him. The stony waste bore no fruit but briers and thorns. The dark ledges of rock thrust themselves above the surface here and there, like the bones of perished monsters. Arid and inhospitable mountain-ranges rose before him, furrowed with dry channels of ancient torrents, white and ghastly as scars on the face of nature. Shifting hills of treacherous sand were heaped like tombs along the horizon. By day, the fierce heat pressed its intolerable burden on the quivering air. No living creature moved on the dumb, swooning earth, but tiny jerboas scuttling through the parched bushes, or lizards vanishing in the clefts of the rock. By the night the jackals prowled and barked in the distance, and the lion made the black ravines echo with his hollow roaring, while a bitter blighting chill followed the fever of the day. Through heat and cold, the Magian moved steadily onward.

Then I saw the gardens and orchards of Damascus, watered by the streams of Abana and Pharpar, with their sloping swards inlaid with bloom, and their thickets of myrrh and roses. I saw the long, snowy ridge of Hermon, and the dark groves of cedars, and the valley of the Jordan, and the blue waters of the Lake of Galilee, and the fertile plain of Esdraelon, and the hills of Ephraim, and the highlands of Judah. Through all these I followed the figure of Artaban moving steadily onward, until he arrived at Bethlehem. And it was the third day after the three Wise Men had come to that place and had found Mary and Joseph, with the young child, Jesus, and had laid their gifts of gold and frankincense and myrrh at his feet.

Then the Other Wise Man drew near, weary, but full of hope, bearing his ruby and his pearl to offer to the King. "For now at last," he said, "I shall surely find him, though I be alone, and later than my brethren. This is the place of which the Hebrew exile told me that the prophets had spoken, and here I shall behold the rising of the great light. But I must inquire about the visit of my brethren, and to what house the star directed them, and to whom they presented their tribute."

The streets of the village seemed to be deserted, and Artaban wondered whether the men had all gone up to the hill-pastures to bring down their sheep. From the open door of a cottage he heard the sound of a woman's voice singing softly. He entered and found a young mother hushing her baby to rest. She told him of the strangers from the far East who had appeared in the village three days ago, and how they said that a star had guided them to the place where Joseph of Nazareth was lodging with his wife and her new-born child, and how they had paid reverence to the child and given him many rich gifts.

"But the travellers disappeared again," she continued, "as suddenly as they had come. We were afraid at the strangeness of their visit. We could not understand it. The man of Nazareth took the child and his mother, and fled away that same night secretly, and it was whispered that they were going to Egypt. Ever since, there has been a spell upon the village; something evil hangs over it. They say that the Roman soldiers are coming from Jerusalem to force a new tax from us, and the men have driven the flocks and herds far back among the hills, and hidden themselves to escape it."

Artaban listened to her gentle, timid speech, and the child in her arms looked up in his face and smiled, stretching out its rosy hands to grasp at the winged circle of gold on his breast. His heart warmed to the touch. It seemed like a greeting of love and trust to one who had journeyed long in loneliness and perplexity, fighting with his own doubts and fears, and following a light that was veiled in clouds.

"Why might not this child have been the promised Prince?" he asked within himself, as he touched its soft cheek. "Kings have been born in lowlier houses than this, and the favorite of the stars may rise even from a cottage. But it has not seemed good to the God of wisdom to reward my search so soon and so easily. The one whom I seek has gone before me; and now I must follow the King to Egypt."

The young mother laid the baby in its cradle, and rose to minister to the wants of the strange guest that fate had brought into her house. She set food before him, the plain fare of peasants, but willingly offered, and therefore full of refreshment for the soul as well as for the body. Artaban accepted it gratefully; and, as he ate, the child fell into a happy slumber, and murmured sweetly in its dreams, and a great peace filled the room.

But suddenly there came the noise of a wild confusion in the streets of the village, a shrieking and wailing of women's voices, a clangour of brazen trumpets and a clashing of swords, and a desperate cry: "The soldiers! The soldiers of Herod! They are killing our children!"

The young mother's face grew white with terror. She clasped her child to her bosom, and crouched motionless in the darkest corner of the room, covering him with the folds of her robe, lest he should wake and cry.

But Artaban went quickly and stood in the doorway of the house. His broad shoulders filled the portal from side to side, and the peak of his white cap all but touched the lintel.

The soldiers came hurrying down the street with bloody hands and dripping swords. At the sight of the stranger in his imposing dress they hesitated with surprise. The captain of the band approached the threshold to thrust him aside. But Artaban did not stir. His face was as calm as though he were watching the stars, and in his eyes there burned that steady radiance before which even the half-tamed hunting leopard shrinks, and the bloodhound pauses in his leap. He held the soldier silently for an instant, and then said in a low voice:

"I am all alone in this place, and I am waiting to give this jewel to the prudent captain who will leave me in peace."

He showed the ruby, glistening in the hollow of his hand like a drop of blood.

The captain was amazed at the splendour of the gem. The pupils of his eyes expanded with desire, and the hard lines of greed wrinkled around his lips. He stretched out his hand and took the ruby.

"March on!" he cried to his men. "There is no child here. The house is empty."

The clamour and the clang of arms passed down the street as the headlong fury of the chase sweeps by the secret covert where the trembling deer is hidden. Artaban re-entered the cottage. He turned his face to the east and prayed, "God of truth, forgive my sin! I have said the thing that is not, to save the life of a child. And two of my gifts are gone. I have spent for man that which was meant for God. Shall I ever be worthy to see the face of the King?"

But the voice of the woman, weeping for joy in the shadow behind him, said very gently, "Because thou hast saved the life of my little one, may the Lord bless thee and keep thee; the Lord make His face to shine upon thee and be gracious unto thee; the Lord lift up His countenance upon thee and give thee peace."

Again there was a silence in the Hall of Dreams, deeper and more mysterious than the first interval, and I understood that the years of Artaban were flowing very swiftly under the stillness, and I caught only a glimpse, here and there, of the river of his life shining through the mist that concealed that course.

I saw him moving among the throngs of men in populous Egypt, seeking everywhere for traces of the household that had come down from Bethlehem, and finding them under the spreading sycamore-trees of Heliopolis, and beneath the walls of the Roman fortress of New Babylon beside the Nile—traces so faint and dim that they vanished before him continually, as footprints on the wet river-sand glisten for a moment with moisture and then disappear.

I saw him again at the foot of the pyramids, which lifted their sharp points into the intense saffron glow of the sunset sky, changeless monuments of the perishable glory and the imperishable hope of man. He looked up into the face of the crouching Sphinx and vainly tried to read the meaning of the calm eyes and smiling mouth. Was it, indeed, the mockery of all effort and all aspiration, as Tigranes had said—the cruel jest of a riddle that has no answer, a search that never can succeed? Or was there a touch of pity and encouragement in that inscrutable smile—a promise that even the defeated should attain a victory, and the disappointed should discover a prize, and the ignorant should be made wise, and the blind should see, and the wandering should come into the haven at last?

I saw him again in an obscure house of Alexandria, taking counsel with a Hebrew rabbi. The venerable man, bending over the rolls of parchment on which the prophecies of Israel were written, read aloud the pathetic words which foretold the sufferings of the promised Messiah—the despised and rejected of men, the man of sorrows and acquainted with grief.

"And remember, my son," said he, fixing his eyes upon the face of Artaban, "the King whom thou seekest is not to be found in a palace, nor among the rich and powerful. If the light of the world and the glory of Israel had been appointed to come with the greatness of earthly splendour, it must have appeared long ago. For no son of Abraham will ever again rival the power which Joseph had in the palaces of Egypt, of the magnificence of Solomon throned between the lions in Jerusalem. But the light for which the world is waiting is a new light, the glory that shall rise out of patient and triumphant suffering. And the kingdom which is to be established forever is a new kingdom, the royalty of unconquerable love.

"I do not know how this shall come to pass, nor how the turbulent kings and peoples of earth shall be brought to acknowledge the Messiah and pay homage to him. But this I know. Those who seek him will do well to look among the poor and the lowly, the sorrowful and the oppressed."

So I saw the Other Wise Man again and again, travelling from place to place, and searching among the people of the dispersion, with whom the little family from Bethlehem might, perhaps, have found a refuge. He passed through countries where famine lay heavy upon the land, and the poor were crying for bread. He made his dwelling in plague-stricken cities where the sick were languishing in the bitter companionship of helpless misery. He visited the oppressed and the afflicted in the gloom of subterranean prisons, and the crowded wretchedness of slave-markets, and the weary toil of galley-ships. In all this populous and intricate world of anguish, though he found none to worship, he found many to help. He fed the hungry, and clothed the naked, and healed the sick, and comforted the captive; and his years passed more swiftly than the weaver's shuttle that flashes back and forth through the loom while the web grows and the pattern is completed.

It seemed almost as if he had forgotten his quest. But once I saw him for a moment as he stood alone at sunrise, waiting at the gate of a Roman prison. He had taken from a secret resting place in his bosom the pearl, the last of his jewels. As he looked at it, a mellower lustre, a soft and iridescent light, full of shifting gleams of azure and rose, trembled upon its surface. It seemed to have absorbed some reflection of the lost sapphire and ruby. So the secret purpose of a noble life draws into itself the memories of past joy and past sorrow. All that has helped it, all that has hindered it, is transfused by a subtle magic into its very essence. It becomes more luminous and precious the longer it is carried close to the warmth of the beating heart.

Then, at last, while I was thinking of this pearl, and of its meaning, I heard the end of the story of the Other Wise Man.

Three-and-thirty years of the life of Artaban had passed away, and he was still a pilgrim and a seeker after the light. His hair, once darker than the cliffs of Zagros, was now white as the wintry snow that covered them. His eyes, that once flashed like flames of fire, were dull as embers smoldering among the ashes.

Worn and weary and ready to die, but still looking for the King, he had come for the last time to Jerusalem. He had often visited the holy city before, and had searched all its lanes and crowded hovels and black prisons without finding any trace of the family of Nazarenes who had fled from Bethlehem long ago. But now it seemed as if he must make one more effort, and something whispered in his heart that, at last, he might succeed.

It was the season of Passover. The city was thronged with strangers. The children of Israel, scattered in far lands, had returned to the Temple for the great feast, and there had been a confusion of tongues in the narrow streets for many days.

But on this day a singular agitation was visible in the multitude. The sky was veiled with a portentous gloom. Currents of excitement seemed to flash through the crowd. A secret tide was sweeping them all one way. The clatter of sandals and the soft, thick sound of thousands of bare feet shuffling over the stones, flowed unceasingly along the street that leads to the Damascus gate.

Artaban joined a group of people from his own country, Parthian Jews who had come up to keep the Passover, and inquired of them the cause of the tumult, and where they were going.

"We are going," they answered, "to the place called Golgotha, outside the city walls, where there is to be an execution. Have you not heard what has happened? Two famous robbers are to be crucified, and with them another, called Jesus of Nazareth, a man who has done many wonderful works among the people, so that they love him greatly. But the priests and elders have said that he must die, because he gave himself out to be the Son of God. And Pilate has sent him to the cross because he said that he was the 'King of the Jews.' "

How strangely these familiar words fell upon the tired heart of Artaban! They had led him for a lifetime over land and sea. And now they came to him mysteriously, like a message of despair. The King had arisen, but he had been denied and cast out. He was about to perish. Perhaps he was already dying. Could it be the same who had been born in Bethlehem thirty-three years ago, at whose birth the star had appeared in heaven, and of whose coming the prophets had spoken?

Artaban's heart beat unsteadily with that troubled, doubtful apprehension which is the excitement of old age. But he said within himself, "The ways of God are stranger than the thoughts of men, and it may be that I shall find the King, at last, in the hands of his enemies, and shall come in time to offer my pearl for his ransom before he dies."

So the old man followed the multitude with slow and painful steps toward the Damascus gate of the city. Just beyond the entrance of the guardhouse a troop of Macedonian soldiers came down the street, dragging a young girl with torn dress and dishevelled hair. As the Magian paused to look at her with compassion, she broke suddenly from the hands of her tormentors, and threw herself at his feet, clasping him around the knees. She had seen his white cap and the winged circle on his breast.

"Have pity on me," she cried, "and save me, for the sake of the God of Purity! I also am a daughter of the true religion which is taught by the Magi. My father was a merchant of Parthis, but he is dead, and I am seized for his debts to be sold as a slave. Save me from worse than death!"

Artaban trembled.

It was the old conflict in his soul, which had come to him in the palm-grove of Babylon and in the cottage at Bethlehem—the conflict between the expectation of faith and the impulse of love. Twice the gift which he had consecrated to the worship of religion had been drawn to the service of humanity. This was the third trial, the ultimate probation, the final and irrevocable choice.

Was it his great opportunity, or his last temptation? He could not tell. One thing only was clear in the darkness of his mind—it was inevitable. And does not the inevitable come from God?

One thing only was sure to his divided heart—to rescue this helpless girl would be a true deed of love. And is not love the light of the soul?

He took the pearl from his bosom. Never had it seemed so luminous, so radiant, so full of tender, living lustre. He laid it in the hand of the slave.

"This is thy ransom, daughter! It is the last of my treasures which I kept for the King."

While he spoke, the darkness of the sky deepened, and shuddering tremors ran through the earth heaving convulsively like the breast of one who struggles with a mighty grief.

The walls of the houses rocked to and fro. Stones were loosened and crashed into the street. Dust clouds filled the air. The soldiers fled in terror, reeling like drunken men. But Artaban and the girl whom he had ransomed crouched helpless beneath the wall of the Praetorium.

What had he to fear? What had he to hope? He had given away the last remnant of his tribute for the King. He had parted with the last hope of finding him. The quest was over, and it had failed. But, even in that thought, accepted and embraced, there was peace. It was not resignation. It was not submission. It was something more profound and searching. He knew that all was well, because he had done the best that he could from day to day. He had been true to the light that had been given to him. He had looked for more. And if he had not found it, if a failure was all that came out of his life, doubtless that was the best that was possible. He had not seen the revelation of "life everlasting, incorruptible and immortal." But he knew that even if he could live his earthly life over again, it could not be otherwise than it had been.

One more lingering pulsation of the earthquake quivered through the ground. A heavy tile, shaken from the roof, fell and struck the old man on the temple. He lay breathless and pale, with his gray head resting on the girl's shoulder, and the blood trickling from the wound. As she bent over him, fearing that he was dead, there came a voice through the twilight, very small and still, like music sounding from a distance, in which the notes are clear but the words are lost. The girl turned to see if someone had spoken from the window above them, but she saw no one.

Then the old man's lips began to move, as if in answer, and she heard him say in the Parthian tongue, "Not so, my Lord! For when saw I thee hungry and fed thee? Or thirsty, and gave thee drink? When saw I thee a stranger, and took thee in? Or naked, and clothed thee? When saw I thee sick or in prison, and came unto thee? Three-and-thirty years have I looked for thee; but I have never seen thy face, nor ministered to thee, my King."

He ceased, and the sweet voice came again. And again the maid heard it, very faint and far away. But now it seemed as though she understood the words: "Verily I say unto thee, inasmuch as thou hast done it unto one of the least of these my brethren, thou hast done it unto me."

A calm radiance of wonder and joy lighted the pale face of Artaban like the first ray of dawn on a snowy mountain-peak. A long breath of relief exhaled gently from his lips.

His journey was ended. His treasures were accepted. The Other Wise Man had found the King.

Christmas in the Heart

Let us now go even unto Bethlehem. — Luke 2:15

To Bethlehem our hearts, star led
    From wanderings far and wild,
Turn to a lowly cattle-shed
    And kneel before the Child.

We come from deserts, pitiless
    With only human pride;
And from the howling wilderness
    Where dread and hate abide.

Touched by his hand we find release
    From heavy griefs and fears:
Our hearts are lifted up with peace
    And purified by tears.

Ah Saviour dear! Thou Holy Child,
    What power is thine to heal
Our broken hearts, our wills, defiled,
    When at thy feet we kneel.

Grant us thy grace no more to roam,
    But, following thee alway,
Find Bethlehem in every home,
    The whole year Christmas Day.

The First Christmas Tree

The day before Christmas, in the year of our Lord 722.

road snow-meadows glistening white along the banks of the river Moselle; steep hill-sides blooming with mystic forget-me-not where the glow of the setting sun cast long shadows down their eastern slope; an arch of clearest, deepest gentian bending overhead; in the center of the aerial garden the walls of the cloister of Pfalzel, steel-blue to the east, violet to the west; silence over all—a gentle, eager, conscious stillness, diffused through the air, as if earth and sky were hushing themselves to hear the voice of the river faintly murmuring down the valley.

In the cloister, too, there was silence at the sunset hour. All day long there had been a strange and joyful stir among the nuns. A breeze of curiosity and excitement had swept along the corridors and through every quiet cell. A famous visitor had come to the convent.

It was Winfried of England, whose name in the Roman tongue was Boniface, and whom men called the Apostle of Germany. A great preacher; a wonderful scholar; but, more than all, a daring traveller, a venturesome pilgrim, a priest of romance.

He had left his home and his fair estate in Wessex; he would not stay in the rich monastery of Nutescelle, even though they had chosen him as the abbot; he had refused a bishopric at the court of King Karl. Nothing would content him but to go out into the wild woods and preach to the heathen.

Through the forests of Hesse and Thuringia, and along the borders of Saxony, he had wandered for years, with a handful of companions, sleeping under the trees, crossing mountains and marshes, now here, now there, never satisfied with ease and comfort, always in love with hardship and danger.

What a man he was! Fair and slight, but straight as a spear and strong as an oaken staff. His face was still young; the smooth skin was bronzed by wind and sun. His gray eyes, clean and kind, flashed like fire when he spoke of his adventures, and of the evil deeds of the false priests with whom he contended.

What tales he had told that day! Not of miracles wrought by sacred relics; not of courts and councils and splendid cathedrals; though he knew much of these things. But to-day he had spoken of long journeyings by sea and land; of perils by fire and flood; of wolves and bears, and fierce snowstorms, and black nights in the lonely forest; of dark altars of heathen gods, and weird, bloody sacrifices, and narrow escapes from murderous bands of wandering savages.

The little novices had gathered around him, and their faces had grown pale and their eyes bright as they listened with parted lips, entranced in admiration, twining their arms about one another's shoulders and holding closely together, half in fear, half in delight. The older nuns had turned from their tasks and paused, in passing by, to hear the pilgrim's story. Too well they knew the truth of what he spoke. Many a one among them had seen the smoke rising from the ruins of her father's roof. Many a one had a brother far away in the wild country to whom her heart went out night and day, wondering if he were still among the living.

But now the excitements of that wonderful day were over; the hour of the evening meal had come; the inmates of the cloister were assembled in the refectory.

On the dais sat the stately Abbess Addula, daughter of King Dagobert, looking a princess indeed, in her purple tunic, with the hood and cuffs of her long white robe trimmed with ermine, and a snowy veil resting like a crown on her silver hair. At her right hand was the honoured guest, and at her left hand her grandson, the young Prince Gregor, a big, manly boy, just returned from school.

The long, shadowing hall, with its dark-brown rafters and beams; the double row of nuns, with their pure veils and fair faces; the ruddy glow of the slanting sunbeams striking upward through the tops of the windows and painting a pink glow high up on the walls—it was all as beautiful as a picture, and as silent. For this was the rule of the cloister, that at the table all should sit in stillness for a little while, and then one should read aloud, while the rest listened.

"It is the turn of my grandson to read to-day," said the abbess to Winfried; "we shall see how much he has learned in the school. Read, Gregor; the place in the book is marked."

The lad rose from his seat and turned the pages of the manuscript. It was a copy of Jerome's version of the Scriptures in Latin, and the marked place was in the letter of St. Paul to the Ephesians—the passage where he describes the preparation of the Christian as a warrior arming for battle. The young voice rang out clearly, rolling the sonorous words, without slip or stumbling, to the end of the chapter.

Winfried listened smiling. "That was bravely read, my son," said he, as the reader paused. "Do you understand what you read?"

"Surely, father," answered the boy. "It was taught me by the masters at Treves; and we have read this epistle from beginning to end, so that I almost know it by heart."

Then he began to repeat the passage, turning away from the page as if to show his skill.

But Winfried stopped him with a friendly lifting of the hand.

"Not so, my son; that was not my meaning. When we pray, we speak to God. When we read, God speaks to us. I ask whether thou hast heard what He has said to thee in the common speech. Come, give us again the message of the warrior and his armor and his battle, in the mother-tongue, so that all can understand it."

The boy hesitated, blushed, stammered; then he came around to Winfried's seat, bringing the book. "Take the book, my father," he cried, "and read it for me. I cannot see the meaning plain, though I love the sound of the words. Religion I know, and the doctrines of our faith, and the life of priests and nuns in the cloister, for which my grandmother designs me, though it likes me little. And fighting I know, and the life of warriors and heroes, for I have read of it in Virgil and the ancients, and heard a bit from the soldiers at Treves; and I would fain taste more of it, for it likes me much. But how the two lives fit together, or what need there is of armor for a clerk in holy orders, I can never see. Tell me the meaning, for if there is a man in all the world that knows it, I am sure it is you."

So Winfried took the book and closed it, clasping the boy's hand with his own.

"Let us first dismiss the others to their vespers," said he, "lest they should be weary."

A sign from the abbess; a chanted benediction; a murmuring of sweet voices and a soft rustling of many feet over the rushes on the floor; the gentle tide of noise flowed out through the doors and ebbed away down the corridors; the three at the head of the table were left alone in the darkening room.

Then Winfried began to translate the parable of the soldier into the realities of life.

At every turn he knew how to flash a new light into the picture out of his own experience. He spoke of the combat with self, and of the wrestling with dark spirits in solitude. He spoke of the demons that men had worshipped for centuries in the wilderness, and whose malice they invoked against the stranger who ventured into the gloomy forest. Gods, they called them, and told weird tales of their dwelling among the impenetrable branches of the oldest trees and in the caverns of the shaggy hills; of their riding on the wind-horses and hurling spears of lightning against their foes. Gods they were not, but foul spirits of the air, rulers of the darkness. Was there not glory and honour in fighting them, in daring their anger under the shield of faith, in putting them to flight with the sword of truth? What better adventure could a brave man ask than to go forth against them, and wrestle with them, and conquer them?

"Look you, my friends," said Winfried, "how sweet and peaceful is this convent to-night! It is a garden full of flowers in the heart of winter; a nest among the branches of a great tree shaken by the winds; a still haven on the edge of a tempestuous sea. And this is what religion means for those who are chosen and called to quietude and prayer and meditation.

"But out yonder in the wide forest, who knows what storms are raving to-night in the hearts of men, though all the woods are still? Who knows what haunts of wrath and cruelty are closed tonight against the advent of the Prince of Peace? And shall I tell you what religion means to those who are called the chosen to dare, and to fight, and to conquer the world for Christ? It means to go against the strongholds of the adversary. It means to struggle to win an entrance for the Master everywhere. What helmet is strong enough for this strife save the helmet of salvation? What breastplate can guard a man gainst these fiery darts but the breastplate of righteousness? What shoes can stand the wear of these journeys but the preparation of the gospel of peace?"

"Shoes?" he cried again, and laughed as if a sudden thought had struck him. He thrust out his foot, covered with a heavy cowhide boot laced high about his leg with thongs of skin.

"Look here—how a fighting man of the cross is shod! I have seen the boots of the Bishop of Tours—white kid, broidered with silk; a day in the bogs would tear them to shreds. I have seen the sandals that the monks use on the highroads—yes, and worn them; ten pair of them have I worn out and thrown away in a single journey. Now I shoe my feet with the toughest hides, hard as iron; no rock can cut them, no branches can tear them. Yet more than one pair of these have I outworn, and many more shall I outwear ere my journeys are ended. And I think, if God is gracious to me, that I shall die wearing them. Better so than in a soft bed with silken coverings. The boots of a warrior, a hunter, a woodsman—these are my preparation of the gospel of peace.

"Come, Gregor," he said, laying his brown hand on the youth's shoulder. "Come, wear the forester's boots with me. This is the life to which we are called. Be strong in the Lord, a hunter of the demons, a subduer of the wilderness, a woodsman of the faith. Come."

The boy's eyes sparkled. He turned to his grandmother. She shook her head vigorously.

"No, father," she said. "Draw not the lad away from my side with these wild words. I need him to help me with my labors, to cheer my old age."

"Do you need him more than the Master does?" asked Winfried. "And will you take the wood that is fit for a bow to make a stick for spinning wool?"

"But I fear for the child. Thy life is too hard for him. He will perish with hunger in the woods."

"Once," said Winfried, smiling, "we were camped on the bank of the river Ohru. The table was set for the morning meal, but my comrades cried that it was empty; the provisions were exhausted; we must go without breakfast, and perhaps starve before we could escape from the wilderness. While they complained, a fish-hawk flew up from the river with flapping wings, and let fall a great pike in the midst of the camp. There was food enough and to spare! Never have I seen the righteous forsaken, nor his seed begging bread."

"But the fierce pagans of the forest," cried the Abbess—"they may pierce the boy with their arrows, or dash out his brains with their axes. He is but a child, too young for the danger and the strife."

"A child in years," replied Winfried, "but a man in spirit. And if the hero must fall early in the battle, he wears the brighter crown, not a leaf withered, not a flower fallen."

The aged princess trembled a little. She drew Gregor close to her side, and laid her hand gently on his brown hair.

"I am not sure that he wants to leave me yet. Besides, there is no horse in the stable to give him, now, and he cannot go as befits the grandson of a king."

Gregor looked straight into her eyes.

"Grandmother," said he, "dear grandmother, if you will not give me a horse to ride with this man of God, I will go with him on foot."

Two years had passed since that Christmas Eve in the cloister of Pfalzel. A little company of pilgrims, less than a score of men, were travelling slowly northward through the wide forest that rolled over the hills of central Germany.

At the head of the band marched Winfried, clad in a tunic of fur, with his long black robe girt high above his waist, so that it might not hinder his stride. His hunter's boots were crusted with snow. Drops of ice sparkled like jewels along the thongs that bound his legs. There were no other ornaments of his dress except the bishop's cross hanging on his breast, and the silver clasp that fastened his cloak about his neck. He carried a strong, tall staff in his hand, fashioned at the top into the form of a cross.

Close beside him, keeping step like a familiar comrade, was the young Prince Gregor. Long marches through the wilderness had stretched his legs and broadened his back, and made a man of him in stature as well as in spirit. His jacket and cap were of wolf-skin, and on his shoulder he carried an axe, with broad, shining blade. He was a mighty woodsman now, and could make a spray of chips fly around him as he hewed his way through the trunk of a pine-tree.

Behind these leaders followed a pair of teamsters, guiding a rude sledge, loaded with food and the equipage of the camp, and drawn by two big, shaggy horses, blowing thick clouds of steam from their frosty nostrils. Tiny icicles hung from the hairs on their lips. Their flanks were smoking. They sank above the fetlocks at every step in the soft snow.

Last of all came the rear guard, armed with bows and javelins. It was no child's play, in those days, to cross Europe afoot.

The weird woodland, sombre and illimitable covered hill and vale, table-land and mountain-peak. There were wide moors where the wolves hunted in packs as if the devil drove them, and tangled thickets where the lynx and the boar made their lairs. Fierce bears lurked among the rocky passes, and had not yet learned to fear the face of man. The gloomy recesses of the forest gave shelter to inhabitants who were still more cruel and dangerous than beasts of prey—outlaws and sturdy robbers and mad were-wolves and bands of wandering pillagers.

The Pilgrim who would pass from the mouth of the Tiber to the mouth of the Rhine must trust in God and keep his arrows loose in the quiver.

The travellers were surrounded by an ocean of trees, so vast, so full of endless billows, that it seemed to be pressing on every side to overwhelm them. Gnarled oaks, with branches twisted and knotted as if in rage, rose in groves like tidal waves. Smooth forests of beech-trees, round and gray, swept over the knolls and slopes of land in a mighty ground-swell. But most of all, the multitude of pines and firs, innumerable and monotonous, with straight, stark trunks, and branches woven together in an unbroken flood of darkest green, crowded through the valleys and over the hills, rising on the highest ridges into ragged crests, like the foaming edge of breakers.

Through this sea of shadows ran a narrow stream of shining whiteness—an ancient Roman road, covered with snow. It was as if some great ship had ploughed through the green ocean long ago, and left behind it a thick, smooth wake of foam. Along this open track the travellers held their way—heavily, for the drifts were deep; warily, for the hard winter had driven many packs of wolves down from the moors.

The steps of the pilgrims were noiseless; but the sledges creaked over the dry snow, and the panting of the horses throbbed through the still air. The pale-blue shadows on the western side of the road grew longer. The sun, declining through its shallow arch, dropped behind the tree-tops. Darkness followed swiftly, as if it had been a bird of prey waiting for this sign to swoop down upon the world.

"Father," said Gregor to the leader, "surely this day's march is done. It is time to rest, and eat, and sleep. If we press onward now, we cannot see our steps; and will not that be against the word of the psalmist David, who bids us not to put confidence in the legs of a man?"

Winfried laughed. "No, my son Gregor," said he, "you have tripped, even now, upon your text. For David said only, 'I take no pleasure in the legs of a man.' And so say I, for I am not minded to spare your legs or mine, until we come farther on our way, and do what must be done this night. Draw your belt tighter, my son, and hew me out this tree that is fallen across the road, for our campground is not here."

The youth obeyed; two of the foresters sprang to help him; and while the soft fir-wood yielded to the stroke of the axes, and the snow flew from the bending branches, Winfried turned and spoke to his followers in a cheerful voice, that refreshed them like wine.

"Courage, brothers, and forward yet a little! The moon will light us presently, and the path is plain. Well know I that the journey is weary; and my own heart wearies also for the home in England, where those I love are keeping feast this Christmas Eve. But we have work to do before we feast to-night. For this is the Yuletide, and the heathen people of the forest are gathered at the thunder-oak of Geismar to worship their god, Thor. Strange things will be seen there, and deeds which make the soul black. But we are sent to lighten their darkness; and we will teach our kinsmen to keep a Christmas with us such as the woodland has never known. Forward, then, and stiffen up the feeble knees!"

A murmur of assent came from the men. Even the horses seemed to take fresh heart. They flattened their backs to draw the heavy loads, and blew the frost from their nostrils as they pushed ahead.

The night grew broader and less oppressive. A gate of brightness was opened secretly somewhere in the sky. Higher and higher swelled the moon-flood, until it poured over the eastern wall of forest into the road. A drove of wolves howled faintly in the distance, but they were receding, and the sound soon died away. The stars sparkled merrily through the stringent air; the small, round moon shone like silver; little breaths of dreaming wind wandered across the pointed fir-tops, as the pilgrims toiled bravely onward, following their streak of light through a labyrinth of darkness.

After a while the road began to open out a little. There were spaces of meadow-land, fringed with alders, behind which a boisterous river ran clashing through spears of ice.

Rude houses of hewn logs appeared in the openings, each one casting a patch of inky shadow upon the snow. Then the travellers passed a larger group of dwellings, all silent and unlighted; and beyond, they saw a great house, with many outbuildings and inclosed courtyards, from which the hounds bayed furiously, and a noise of stamping horses came from the stalls. But there was no other sound of life. The fields around lay naked to the moon. They saw no man, except that once, on a path that skirted the farther edge of a meadow, three dark figures passed them, running very swiftly.

Then the road plunged again into a dense thicket, traversed it, and climbing to the left, emerged suddenly upon a glade, round and level except at the northern side, where a hillock was crowned with a huge oak-tree. It towered above the heath, a giant with contorted arms, beckoning the host of lesser trees. "Here," cried Winfried, as his eyes flashed and his hand lifted his heavy staff, "here is the Thunder-Oak; and here the cross of Christ shall break the hammer of the false god Thor."

Withered leaves still clung to the branches of the oak; torn and faded banners of the departed summer. The bright crimson of autumn had long since disappeared, bleached away by the storms and the cold. But to-night these tattered remnants of glory were red again: ancient blood-stains against the dark-blue sky. For an immense fire had been kindled in front of the tree. Tongues of ruddy flame, fountains of ruby sparks, ascended through the spreading limbs and flung a fierce illumination upward and around. The pale, pure moonlight that bathed the surrounding forests was quenched and eclipsed here. Not a beam of it sifted through the branches of the oak. It stood like a pillar of cloud between the still light of heaven and the crackling, flashing fire of earth.

But the fire itself was invisible to Winfried and his companions. A great throng of people were gathered around it in a half-circle, their backs to the open glade, their faces toward the oak. Seen against that glowing background, it was but the silhouette of a crowd, vague, black, formless, mysterious.

The travellers paused for a moment at the edge of the thicket, and took counsel together.

"It is the assembly of the tribe," said one of the foresters, "the great night of the council. I heard of it three days ago, as we passed through one of the villages. All who swear by the old gods have been summoned. They will sacrifice a steed to the god of war, and drink blood, and eat horse-flesh to make them strong. It will be at the peril of our lives if we approach them. At least we must hide the cross, if we would escape death."

"Hide me no cross," cried Winfried, lifting his staff, "for I have come to show it, and to make these blind folk see its power. There is more to be done here to-night than the slaying of a steed, and a greater evil to be stayed than the shameful eating of meat sacrificed to idols. I have seen it in a dream. Here the cross must stand and be our message."

At his command the sledge was left in the border of the wood, with two of the men to guard it, and the rest of the company moved forward across the open ground. They approached unnoticed, for all the multitude were looking intently toward the fire at the foot of the oak.

Then Winfried's voice rang out, "Hail, you sons of the forest! A stranger claims the warmth of your fire in the winter night."

Swiftly, and as with a single motion, a thousand eyes were bent upon the speaker. The semicircle opened silently in the middle; Winfried entered with his followers; it closed again behind them.

Then, as they looked round the curving ranks, they saw that the hue of the assemblage was not black, but white—dazzling, radiant, solemn. White, the robes of the women clustered together at the points of the wide crescent; white, the glittering breastplates of the warriors standing in close ranks; white, the fur mantles of the aged men who held the central place in the circle; white, with the shimmer of silver ornaments and the purity of lamb's-wool, the raiment of a little group of children who stood close by the fire; white, with awe and fear, the faces of all who looked at them; and over all the flickering, dancing radiance of the flames played and glimmered like a faint, vanishing tinge of blood on snow.

The only figure untouched by the glow was the old priest, Hunrad, with his long, spectral robe, flowing hair and beard, and dead-pale face, who stood with his back to the fire and advanced slowly to meet the strangers.

"Who are you? Whence come you, and what seek you here?"

"Your kinsman am I, of the German brotherhood," answered Winfried, "and from England, beyond the sea, have I come to bring you a greeting from that land, and a message from the All-Father, whose servant I am."

"Welcome, then," said Hunrad. "Welcome, kinsman, and be

silent; for what passes here is too high to wait, and must be done before the moon crosses the middle heaven, unless, indeed, you have some sign or token from the gods. Can you work miracles?"

The question came sharply, as if a sudden gleam of hope had flashed through the tangle of the old priest's mind. But Winfried's voice sank lower and a cloud of disappointment passed over his face as he replied: "No, miracles have I never wrought, though I have heard of many; but the All-Father has given no power to my hands save such as belongs to common man."

"Stand still, then, you common man," said Hunrad, scornfully, "and behold what the gods have called us hither to do. This night is the death-night of the sun-god, Baldur the Beautiful, beloved of gods and men. This night is the hour of darkness and the power of winter, of sacrifice and mighty fear. This night the great Thor, the god of thunder and war, to whom this oak is sacred, is grieved for the death of Baldur, and angry with this people because they have forsaken his worship. Long is it since an offering has been laid upon his altar, long since the roots of his holy tree have been fed with blood. Therefore its leaves have withered before the time, and its boughs are heavy with death. Therefore the Slavs and the Wends have beaten us in battle. Therefore the harvests have failed, and the wolf-hordes have ravaged the folds, and the strength has departed from the bow, and the wood of the spear has broken, and the wild boar has slain the huntsman. Therefore the plague has fallen on our dwellings, and the dead are more than the living in all our villages. Answer me, you people, are not these things true?"

A hoarse sound of approval ran through the circle. A chant, in which the voices of the men and women blended, like the shrill wind in the pine-trees above the rumbling thunder of a waterfall, rose and fell in rude cadences.

O Thor, the Thunderer,
Mighty and merciless,
Spare us from smiting!
Heave not thy hammer,
Angry, against us;
Plague not thy people.
Take from our treasure
Richest of ransom.
Silver we send thee,
Jewels and javelins,
Goodliest garments,
All our possessions,
Priceless, we proffer.
Sheep will we slaughter,
Steeds will we sacrifice;
Bright blood shall bathe thee,
O tree of Thunder,
Life-floods shall lave thee,
Strong wood of wonder.
Mighty, have mercy,
Smite us no more,
Spare us and save us,
Spare us, Thor! Thor!

With two great shouts the song ended, and a stillness followed so intense that the crackling of the fire was heard distinctly. The old priest stood silent for a moment. His shaggy brows swept down over his eyes like ashes quenching flame. Then he lifted his face and spoke.

"None of these things will please the god. More costly is the offering that shall cleanse your sin, more precious the crimson dew that shall send new life into his holy tree of blood. Thor claims your dearest and your noblest gift."

Hunrad moved nearer to the group of children who stood watching the fire and the swarms of spark-serpents darting upward. They had heeded none of the priest's words, and did not notice now that he approached them, so eager were they to see which fiery snake would go highest among the oak branches. Foremost among them, and most intent on the pretty game, was a boy like a sunbeam, slender and quick, with blithe brown eyes and laughing lips. The priest's hand was laid upon his shoulder. The boy turned and looked up in his face.

"Here," said the old man, with his voice vibrating as when a thick rope is strained by a ship swinging from her moorings. "Here is the chosen one, the eldest son of the Chief, the darling of the people. Hearken, Bernhard, will you go to Valhalla, where the heroes dwell with the gods, to bear a message to Thor?"

The boy answered, swift and clear, "Yes, priest, I will go if my father bids me. Is it far away? Shall I run quickly? Must I take my bow and arrows for the wolves?"

The boy's father, the Chieftan Gundhar, standing among his bearded warriors, drew his breath deep, and leaned so heavily on the handle of his spear that the wood cracked. And his wife, Irma, bending forward from the ranks of women, pushed the golden hair from her forehead with one hand. The other dragged at the silver chain about her neck until the rough links pierced her flesh, and the red drops fell unheeded on her breast.

A sigh passed through the crowd, like the murmur of the forest before the storm breaks. Yet no one spoke save Hunrad. "Yes, my Prince, both bow and spear shall you have, for the way is long, and you are a brave huntsman. But in darkness you must journey for a little space, and with eyes blindfolded. Do you fear?"

"I fear not," said the boy, "neither darkness, nor the great bear, nor the were-wolf. For I am Gundhar's son, and the defender of my folk."

Then the priest led the child in his raiment of lamb's-wool to a broad stone in front of the fire. He gave him his little bow tipped with silver, and his spear with shining head of steel. He bound the child's eyes with a white cloth, and bade him kneel beside the stone with his face to the east. Unconsciously the wide arc of spectators drew inward toward the center, as the ends of the bow draw together when the cord is stretched. Winfried moved noiselessly until he stood close behind the priest.

The old man stooped to lift a black hammer of stone from the ground—the sacred hammer of the god Thor. Summoning all the strength of his withered arms, he swung it high in the air. It poised for an instant above the child's fair head—then turned to fall.

One keen cry shrilled out from where the women stood: "Me! Take me! Not Bernhard!"

The flight of the mother toward her child was swift as the falcon's swoop. But swifter still was the hand of the deliverer.

Winfried's heavy staff thrust mightily against the hammer's handle as it fell. Sideways it glanced from the old man's grasp, and the black stone, striking on the altar's edge, split in twain. A shout of awe and joy rolled along the living circle. The branches of the oak shivered. The flames leaped higher. As the shout died away the people saw the lady Irma, with her arms clasped round her child, and above them, on the altar-stone, Winfried, his face shining like the face of an angel.

A swift mountain flood rolling down its channel; a huge rock tumbling from the hill-side and falling in mid-stream: the baffled waters broken and confused, pausing in their flow, dash high against the rock, foaming and murmuring, with divided impulse, uncertain whether to turn to the right or the left.

Even so Winfried's bold deed fell into the midst of the thoughts and passions of the council. They were at a standstill. Anger and wonder, reverence and joy and confusion surged through the crowd. They knew not which way to move: to resent the intrusion of the stranger as an insult to their gods, or to welcome him as the rescuer of their prince.

The old priest crouched by the altar, silent. Conflicting counsels troubled the air. Let the sacrifice go forward; the gods must be appeased. Nay, the boy must not die; bring the chieftain's best horse and slay it in his stead; it will be enough; the holy tree loves the blood of horses. Not so, there is a better counsel yet; seize the stranger whom the gods have led hither as a victim and make his life pay the forfeit of his daring.

The withered leaves on the oak rustle and whispered overhead. The fire flared and sank again. The angry voices clashed against each other and fell like opposing waves. Then the chieftain Gundhar struck the earth with his spear and gave his decision.

"All have spoken, but none are agreed. There is no voice of the council. Keep silence now, and let the stranger speak. His words shall give us judgment, whether he is to live or to die."

Winfried lifted himself high upon the altar, drew a roll of parchment from his bosom, and began to read.

"A letter from the great Bishop of Rome, who sits on a golden throne, to the people of the forest, Hessians and Thuringians, Franks and Saxons. *In nomin Domini, sanctae et individuae Trinitatis, amen!*"

A murmur of awe ran through the crowd. "It is the sacred tongue of the Romans; the tongue that is heard and understood by the wise men of every land. There is magic in it. Listen!"

Winfried went on to read the letter, translating it into the speech of the people.

"We have sent unto you our Brother Boniface, and appointed him your bishop, that he may teach you the only true faith, and baptise you, and lead you back from the ways of error to the path of salvation. Hearken to him in all things like a father. Bow your hearts to his teaching. He comes not for earthly gain, but for the gain of your souls. Depart from evil words. Worship not the false gods, for they are devils. Offer no more bloody sacrifices, nor eat the flesh of horses, but do as our Brother Boniface commands you. Build a house for him that he may dwell among you, and a church where you may offer your prayers to the only living God, the Almighty King of Heaven."

It was a splendid message: proud, strong, peaceful, loving. The dignity of the words imposed mightily upon the hearts of the people. They were quieted as men who have listened to a lofty strain of music.

"Tell us, then," said Gundhar, "what is the word that you bring to us from the Almighty? What is your counsel for the tribes of the woodland on this night of sacrifice?"

"This is the word, and this is the counsel," answered Winfried. "Not a drop of blood shall fall to-night, save that which pity has drawn from the breast of your princess, in love for her child. Not a life shall be blotted out in the darkness to-night; but the great shadow of the tree which hides you from the light of heaven shall be swept away. For this is the birth-night of the white Christ, son of the All-Father, and Saviour of mankind. Fairer is He than Baldur the Beautiful, greater than Odin the Wise, kinder than Freya the Good. Since He has come to earth the bloody sacrifice must cease. The dark Thor, on whom you vainly call, is dead. Deep in the shades of Niffelheim he is lost forever. His power in the world is broken. Will you serve a helpless god? See, my brothers, you call this tree his oak. Does he dwell here? Does he protect it?"

A troubled voice of assent rose from the throng. The people stirred uneasily. Women covered their eyes. Hunrad lifted his head and muttered hoarsely, "Thor! Take vengeance! Thor!"

Winfried beckoned to Gregor. "Bring the axes, yours and one for me. Now, young woodsman, show your craft! The king-tree of the forest must fall, and swiftly, or all is lost!"

The two men took their places facing each other, one on each side of the oak. Their cloaks were flung aside, their heads bare. Carefully they felt the ground with their feet, seeking a firm grip of the earth. Firmly they grasped the axes and swung the shining blades.

"Tree-god!" cried Winfried. "Are you angry? Thus we smite you!"

"Tree-god!" answered Gregor. "Are you mighty? Thus we fight you."

Clang! Clang! The alternate strokes beat time upon the hard, ringing wood. The axe-heads glittered in their rhythmic flight, like fierce eagles circling about their quarry.

The broad flakes of wood flew from the deepening gashes in the sides of the oak. The huge trunk quivered. There was a shuddering in the branches. Then the great wonder of Winfried's life came to pass.

Out of the stillness of the winter night, a mighty rushing noise sounded overhead.

Was it the ancient gods on their white battlesteeds, with their black hounds of wrath and their arrows of lightning, sweeping through the air to destroy their foes?

A strong, whirling wind passed over the tree-tops. It gripped the oak by its branches and tore it from the roots. Backward it fell, like a ruined tower, groaning and crashing as it split asunder in four great pieces.

Winfried let his axe drop, and bowed his head for a moment in the presence of almighty power.

Then he turned to the people, "Here is the timber," he cried, "already felled and split for your new building. On this spot shall rise a chapel to the true God and his servant St. Peter.

"And here," said he, as his eyes fell on a young fir-tree, standing straight and green, with its top pointing toward the stars, amid the divided ruins of the fallen oak, "here is the living tree, with no stain of blood upon it, that shall be the sign of your new worship. See how it points to the sky? Call it the tree of the Christ-child. Take it up and carry it to the chieftain's hall. You shall go no more into the shadows of the forest to keep your feasts with secret rites of shame. You shall keep them at home, with laughter and songs and rites of love. The Thunder-Oak has fallen, and I think the day is coming when there shall not be a home in all Germany where the children are not gathered around the green fir-tree to rejoice in the birth-night of Christ."

So they took the little fir from its place, and carried it in joyous procession to the edge of the glade, and laid it on the sledge. The horses tossed their heads and drew their load bravely, as if the new burden had made it lighter.

When they came to the house of Gundhar, he bade them throw open the doors of the hall and set the tree in the midst of it. They kindled lights among the branches until it seemed to be tangled full of fire-flies. The children encircled it, wondering, and the sweet odour of the balsam filled the house.

Then Winfried stood beside the chair of Gundhar, on the dais at the end of the hall, and told the story of Bethlehem; of the babe in the manger, of the shepherds on the hills, of the host of angels and their midnight song. All the people listened, charmed into stillness.

But the boy Bernhard, on Irma's knee, folded in her soft arms, grew restless as the story lengthened, and began to prattle softly at his mother's ear.

"Mother," whispered the child, "why did you cry out so loud, when the priest was going to send me to Valhalla?"

"Oh, hush, my child," answered the mother, and pressed him closer to her side.

"Mother," whispered the boy again, laying his finger on the stains upon her breast, "see, your dress is red! What are these stains? Did some one hurt you?"

The mother closed his mouth with a kiss. "Dear, be still, and listen!"

The boy obeyed. His eyes were heavy with sleep. But he heard the last words of Winfried as he spoke of the angelic messengers, flying over the hills of Judea and singing as they flew. The child wondered and dreamed and listened. Suddenly his face grew bright. He put his lips close to Irma's cheek again.

"Oh, mother!" he whispered very low. "Do not speak. Do you hear them? Those angels have come back again. They are singing now behind the tree."

And some say that it was true; but others say that it was only Gregor and his companions at the lower end of the hall, chanting their Christmas hymn:

> *All glory be to God on high,*
> *And on the earth be peace!*
> *Good-will, henceforth, from heaven to men*
> *Begin and never cease.*

Keeping Christmas

Romans 14:6: He that regardeth the day, regardeth it unto the Lord.

 t is a good thing to observe Christmas day. The mere marking of times and seasons, when men agree to stop work and make merry together, is a wise and wholesome custom. It helps one to feel the supremacy of the common life over the individual life. It reminds a man to set his own little watch, now and then, by the great clock of humanity which runs on sun time.

But there is a better thing than the observance of Christmas day, and that is, keeping Christmas.

Are you willing to forget what you have done for other people, and to remember what other people have done for you; to ignore what the world owes you, and to think what you owe the world; to put your rights in the background, and your duties in the middle distance, and your chances to do a little more than your duty in the foreground; to see that your fellow-men are just as real as you are, and try to look behind their faces to their hearts, hungry for joy; to own that probably the only good reason for your existence is not what you are going to get out of life, but what you are going to give to life; to close your book of complaints against the management of the universe, and look

around you for a place where you can sow a few seeds of happiness—
are you willing to do these things even for a day? Then you can keep
Christmas.

Are you willing to stoop down and consider the needs and the
desires of little children; to remember the weakness and loneliness of
people who are growing old; to stop asking how much your friends
love you, and ask yourself whether you love them enough; to bear in
mind the things that other people have to bear on their hearts; to try
to understand what those who live in the same house with you really
want, without waiting for them to tell you; to trim your lamp so that
it will give more light and less smoke, and to carry it in front so that
your shadow will fall behind you; to make a grave for your ugly
thoughts, and a garden for your kindly feelings, with the gate open—
are you willing to do these things even for a day? Then you can keep
Christmas.

Are you willing to believe that love is the strongest thing in the
world—stronger than hate, stronger than evil, stronger than death—
and that the blessed life which began in Bethlehem nineteen hundred
years ago is the image and brightness of the Eternal Love? Then you
can keep Christmas.

And if you keep it for a day, why not always?

But you can never keep it alone.

A WORD TO THE READER

Thinking and dreaming over the reality of the first Christmas and how Jesus of Nazareth came to be born in Bethlehem, I was given this story.

It does not claim to be a historical record. It is a picture drawn by imagination looking for the truth. But there is nothing here that is out of harmony with the Gospels, nothing that does not belong to the holy land and time when these things came to pass. I know the long trail between Galilee and Judea by foot and heart. Thus the story seems to me true.

It is also a new story because it answers three natural questions that have never before been answered. It tries to tell the human side of a divine event.

So I offer it to you, reader, in all sincerity; and to Him who is the Son of God and the Son of Man, in all adoration.

Even unto Bethlehem

On the Hill above Nazareth

On the high round top of the hill above Nazareth, the village carpenter, Joseph the son of Jacob, was resting in the evening with his young wife Mary. She was very fair and lovely in the habitual dress of a maid of Bethlehem — dark-red bodice, blue skirt, and long blue cloak, a white veil covering her light golden hair but not her deep blue eyes and thoughtful face. Her husband was a man of middle age,

brown-eyed, brown-bearded, wearing his working clothes and carpenter's apron.

The grass beneath them was dry and warm, for it was October; the drought of summer had left the fields parched; the early rains had not yet fallen. The wide rolling world around them was golden-brown, like the pale color of a topaz. Valley and plain and mountain-side lay bathed in the long radiance of the sinking sun.

It was a favorite time and place with these new-wedded lovers. The solitude and silence brought them closer to each other. The glorious view opened their hearts to the large and tranquil thoughts in which our little life expands to a nobler meaning, faith seems easier, and love more rich and pure—a pulse of the very heart of nature.

Northward, snowy Hermon, great Sheikh of Mountains, towered in the rosy gold. Eastward, the rolling hills of Moab were a long bulwark beyond Jordan. Southward, across the Plain of Esdraelon, Samaria was a tumbled sea of crests and ridges. Westward, the wide open waters of the Mediterranean flashed in the sunlight or darkened in the shadow of a passing cloud.

The man repeated a verse from the Psalter in his deep drawling Galilean voice.

"I will lift up mine eyes unto the hills, from whence cometh my help."

The woman answered, in the clearer accent of the Judean folk.

"My help cometh from the Lord, which made heaven and earth."

Her blue eyes grew misty with tears—not tears of grief, but of that mysterious restlessness known only to a woman when she thinks of her time of supreme trial in bringing a new life into the world.

"Help?" she murmured. "God knows I shall need help, if the words the angel spoke to me in my dream are true. I am only a country girl. Why should I be chosen to bear the hope of Israel, the seed of

David, the son of the Most High? And the time comes on so fast! Here it is, long past the second harvest; and by the turn of winter my baby must be born. How can I wait for it? How can I face it, husband?"

The bearded man, grown heavy and slow in his life of hard manual toil, laid his big brown hand, calloused and toughened by the use of saw and plane, mallet and chisel, very gently on the slender hand of his girl wife as if to comfort her. He was slow in speech as well as thought.

"Be not afraid, my Mary," he said. "It is all right."

Then he tried to turn her mind away from herself. He pointed down to the great Roman highway which wound among the hills far below them—the road from Damascus to Acca where the white-sailed ships lay waiting in the harbor to carry the commerce of the East across the blue Mediterranean.

"Look, wife," he said, "there goes the third long caravan since we have been sitting here. Busy times!"

The great world distantly went by in a rich parade before the eyes of the rustic couple.

Roman soldiers in glittering ranks, armored and helmeted, with bright eagle-standards shining above their rows of spears. Proud horsemen on their Arab stallions. Rich merchants and noblemen in their cushioned litters. Rumbling chariots of brass and gilded wood. Gaily-decorated mules, their collars studded with turquoises and their pack-saddles heaped with crates and boxes. Pattering asses moving under their huge loads like patient curious insects. Scornful, ungainly camels swaying silently along on their padded feet, fastened one to another by ropes or jingling chains, like lines of barges in a tow, laden with corn from the Hauran, silks and swords from Damascus, spices and fragrant woods from Arabia, sweet fruits from the orchards and gardens of Galilee, ornaments and jewels and carven-work from the

Greek cities of the Decapolis. All the wealth and splendour of the earth poured along that paved road with its three tracks, each twelve feet wide, divided by upright stones.

On the southern track the eastward flow was scanty just now, mostly of unladen beasts and their drivers, going back to fetch another load, and perhaps one or two convoys of gold and silver money, heavily guarded by soldiers. On the central track, riders and foot-travellers met and passed, going and coming. On the northern track, the westward tide was in full flood. The ancient Orient, mother of luxury and proud indulgence, poured her varied riches toward the bright highway of the sea, that swift ships might bear her merchandise to the eager new markets of Greece and Italy, Gaul and Spain.

Yet on the very edge of all this gleaming, foaming turbulence of world-trade—on the edge of it and above it—the hills and valleys of fair Galilee lay peaceful and secluded. A fertile land and happy; a rustic land and old-fashioned; inhabited by a simple, warm-hearted people who cultivated their gardens and orchards, reaped their crops of wheat and barley, fed their flocks in green pastures, and caught fish in the still waters of the Lake-that-is-shaped-like-a-Harp.

From father to son the village crafts of the carpenter, the smith, the weaver, the potter, were handed down. From mother to daughter the household arts of spinning and sewing, butter-making and bread-baking were transmitted.

The teachers spoke a plainer doctrine. In the synagogues a simple truth was preached. There was more poetry and faith in Galilee than in all Jerusalem and the rich cities of Judah.

Of this plain, hard-working, high-minded folk were Joseph and Mary. They were content in poverty, since they were enriched in soul by the promise made of old to the people of Israel. They were happy in obscurity and not downcast, since they knew that they were of the house and lineage of David, from whose royal seed the Messiah was to come. They could let the pomp and vanity of the world stream by below them without an envious thought.

So they watched the amethyst colors deepening on the far mountains of Samaria and Moab, and listened to the larks rising and falling on their fountains of song in the last glow of sunset, and saw the gold and lilac crocuses of autumn blossoming sparsely in the short grass. This provision of beauty was enough for them. With their love, their peace, their great secret hope, they were well-content.

"Come," said Joseph, "the air grows colder. Let us go down to our house. You must not take a chill."

"Yes," answered Mary, "it is time to go home. I will light a fire on the hearth. I hope we can live there quietly until my son is born. It is a friendly house, though it is so small; I can wait patiently there. I am the handmaid of the Lord; be it unto me according to his word."

So they went down the hill, not by the short steep path, but by a longer, easier one. They came to their home on the outskirts of the village, a low cottage of gray stone with the workshop beside it, in a little garden of silvery olive-trees.

The small Egyptian windows toward the street were dark; the wooden door was fastened on the inside with bolts of wood. Joseph drew them back with his key. They crossed the threshold. Mary kindled a bundle of sticks on the hearthstone, and lit a lamp of oil on the table. The whole house was full of light. From the open window of the workshop came a pleasant smell of fresh-hewn planks and wood-shavings. The carpenter and his wife were at home.

In the Carpenter's House

Of all the handicrafts in the world, there is none cleaner, pleasanter, and more fragrant than that of the carpenter. He works with friendly materials. If he knows it well enough and can feel its qualities, it yields readily to his working and takes the outward shape of his thought— chair or table or bed, window-frame or shelf or beam.

Well-seasoned lumber he wants, that it may not warp. Knots and cross-grains trouble him, like original sin in man; but he takes note carefully, and avoids or conquers them. He judges his material with the eye before he measures it with square and foot-rule. His mind guides his fingers; his fingers fit his tools; his tools work his will in the wood.

What good odors rise around him as he labors! From each tree its own fragrance; the resinous smell of the terebinth and the cypress; the delicate scent of the wild-olive with its smooth, curly texture; the faint, dry sweetness of the orange-yellow acacia with its darker heart; the clean odor of the oak with its hard, solid grain; and on rare days, the aromatic perfume of some precious piece of the cedar of Lebanon, king of trees.

Joseph, the carpenter of Nazareth, was proud of his trade. He loved it. At the beginning of December, on a cloudy morning, he was in shop making a wedding-chest for the daughter of a rich neighbour. The long box of durable shittim-wood was well smoothed with the plane and firmly recessed with pins of oak; and now on the lid Joseph was working an ornament. With gouge and chisel and file, he wrought his design; not of birds or beasts or human figures, for that would have been against the Jewish tradition; but a graceful pattern of a vine with curving branches, broad leaves, and rich clusters of grapes. That was permitted by law. Was it not even a sacred sign and emblem? Joseph hummed an old song as he carved:

> Blessed is every one that feareth the Lord,
> And walketh in his ways.
> Thou shalt eat the labor of thy hands;
> Happy shalt thou be.
> Thy wife shall be as a fruitful vine,
> Planted within thy house.

He stood ankle-deep in shavings, absorbed in his task. From the doorway Mary called to him. He looked up.

"Husband, I am going to the village fountain to fill our water-jar. It is empty. There are curious rumors going about among the neighbors. All the other women will be at the fountain. They will tell me the news."

"They surely will," answered the man. "They always know all that is going on—and sometimes more! But go carefully, beloved. Do not strain to lift the heavy jar."

Gathered around the clear flowing spring, beneath its arch of stone beyond the market-place, Mary found a little crowd of women and girls, filling their jars and pitchers, and talking volubly together. From them she gathered all the gossip. At last came the bit of news which she had feared.

They looked at her curiously and with those sidelong glances which women always wear when they have been talking about you before you came. But they were kind to her. There was even a shade of pity in their look as they told the news which had a special meaning for her. They helped her to lift her jar of water and balance it on her shoulder. Then she walked home with faltering steps under her burden.

Joseph met her at the door. He took the jar from her shoulder and set it within the house.

"What is it?" he asked. "Why are you so sad?"

"It is bad news, Joseph," she answered, "and it must be true, because it was the wife of the teacher who told me. A decree has gone out from the great heathen man at Rome—the one they call Caesar—that all the world must be enrolled for the payment of a new tax. The governor of Syria has proclaimed it, and that vile king, Herod the Idumean, has ordered it to be done. All the people must be written down in the lists in their own cities, according to Jewish law, by tribes and families. Oh, Joseph, do you see what that means for us? We must go to Bethlehem, the city of the family of David. I am terribly afraid of that long, hard journey now, with my time so near. What if we should run into something dangerous? What if an accident should befall me? What if I should lose the child I carry, the hope of Israel? I could not bear it. Ah, woe is me! Woe is me!"

She was shaken with grief as she sank upon the bench. The tears rolled down her cheeks, splashing on her dark-red bodice and long blue cloak. The white veil which covered her hair was thrown back in disorder. She was the picture of dismay and sorrow.

Joseph kneeled beside her, distressed and bewildered so that he could hardly speak.

"Listen, dear heart," he stammered. "It may not be so bad. You speak of Jewish law—but this is a decree of Roman law. Perhaps there is a way out! Our names might be enrolled here in Nazareth—I was born in Galilee—then we could send them to Bethlehem to be registered. What do you think? My friend Matthew in Capernaum is an officer for the Romans—a tax-gatherer—I will go and ask him about it. It is not too far to Capernaum! I shall be back soon. Don't be afraid, my wife."

So Mary was a little comforted and dried her tears. Joseph took his staff and a loaf of bread, and set out for the Lake-that-is-shaped-like-a-Harp.

In his absence, Mary was at first very restless and anxious about the result of his journey. On the second day, she went into the synagogue and took her place with the women behind the lattice, in the enclosure assigned to them. The speaker for that day was a stranger, a rabbi from Jerusalem. Standing, according to the custom, he read from the book of the Prophet Micah.

"But thou, Bethlehem Ephratah, which art little among the thousands of Judah, out of thee shall One come forth that is to be Ruler in Israel; whose goings forth are from of old, from eternity. Therefore will he give them up until the time that she who travaileth hath brought forth; then the residue of his brethren shall return unto the children of Israel."

Strange words, thought Mary; could they have any special meaning for her? "Bethlehem"? "She who travaileth"? The "Ruler in Israel"? Here was a matter that touched her closely.

She listened intently while the preacher, taking his seat now on the bema as was the custom, began to explain the Scripture that he had read.

"Bethlehem was David's city. Nowhere else than in this little town can the Messiah, who is to be the son of David, come into the world. 'She who travaileth' is not named. But even now some unknown daughter of Israel may be carrying the Redeemer of God's people hidden under her breast. Wait then, ye faithful, wait patiently, and look with hope to Bethlehem. To Bethlehem first, to Bethlehem only!"

Mary, standing quietly among the women, with her veil drawn down to hide her face, was thrilled to the heart, uplifted, transfigured with a strong joy. Her prayer in time of trouble had been heard. A word direct from heaven had come to her. She herself was the "unknown daughter of Israel."

Her fear vanished. Her path shone clear before her. She lifted her veil from her face, and walked home, full of courage and vigor, determined in her duty.

Late that evening Joseph returned from Capernaum, dusty and weary.

"Good news," he cried. "Matthew can arrange it. You can be enrolled here. I may have to go to Bethlehem, but you will stay here, dearest!"

"No, my husband," she answered quietly. "My mind has been changed. A message has come to me straight from heaven. All my fears are gone. My son shall be born in the place where the prophet has foretold his coming. For me, even more than for you, this journey is necessary. You shall never leave me nor forsake me. No harm will come to me. The power of the Most High has overshadowed me. Let us go even unto Bethlehem. To-morrow I will send a letter to my cousin Elizabeth to meet us there. In Bethlehem it must be."

The Long Long Way to Bethlehem

The preparations for the journey were simple, but it took some time to make them. The affairs of Joseph must be put in order; his promised work delivered, his few debts paid, his small dues collected. With part of his savings, he bought an ass, very small and old and thin, and therefore cheap.

"He is not much to look at," said Joseph, "poor old Thistles! But he is patient and tough; and he picks his living along the road. He can carry you over the rough places. The whole way on foot would wear you out."

The aged man who sold the donkey to Joseph had been a peddler, travelling around the country with earthenware for sale. For these journeys in all kinds of weather he had provided himself with a big mantle of goat's-hair, so closely woven that it was waterproof. This also he wished to sell, since his travelling days were done.

This will be the very thing for my wife, thought Joseph. *It is not pretty; but the cold winter rains are coming on, and we may have to sleep out at night before we get to Bethlehem. This will be like a little tent for her.*

So Joseph bought it with two of the few silver coins that were left in his purse. Mary laughed when she tried it on over her pretty blue cloak.

"It makes me look like an Ethiopian woman," she said.

"Little matter how it looks," said her husband, "if it only keeps you dry and warm."

Other clothing too would be needed, particularly some long linen bands for swaddling a baby. These Mary prepared with her own fingers, taking great pains with them and embroidering Hebrew letters on them in red and blue threads.

Joseph fastened a sharp iron spike on the end of his heaviest staff, so that it would serve as a weapon if any wild beast attacked them. Last of all, a supply of bread must be baked, some thin strips of meat dried and salted, a bag of lentils provided, and a small earthen pot to cook them in — also a cup and a water-bottle. So the outfit was completed and the time of their departure was at hand: the third week of December.

There were three ways from Galilee to the high lands of Judea. One went by the west along the sea-coast and the plain of Sharon. But that was frequented by rowdy foreigners and led through rich heathen seaports, full of abominations. The straightest and shortest road crossed the plain of Esdraelon into the mountains of Samaria, and so by Shechem and Bethel to Jerusalem. But it was a steep road and the Samaritans who lived along that line were rude and churlish folk and the Jews had no dealings with them. The third route descended into the Jordan Valley, followed the east bank of the river, and went up from Jericho into the hills. Perhaps it was a bit round-about, but it was fairly level and for a good part of the way it was the warmest of the three routes. This was their choice.

So they shut their small stone house and left it in charge of a neighbour; said good-bye to peaceful Nazareth nestling in its green hollow among the hills; and went down the open road to their great adventure.

There were no angelic wings to bear them up and carry them over the rough places, lest Mary should bruise her foot against a stone. No rich traveller rolling by offered them a lift in his chariot; they were too humble and poor for that courtesy. Nor was there any miracle to remove the hardships or shorten the weary miles of the long, long way. Step after step they must measure the hundred miles, with only poor little Thistles to carry the scanty luggage and to let Mary ride on his back now and then, when she was too tired to put one foot before the other.

Past the village of Endor below the Mount Tabor where Saul's witch once lived, past Shunem where Elisha's generous hostess built a room for him on the wall of her house and called it a prophet's chamber, the pilgrims trudged along until they came to a quiet nook on the lower slope of Little Hermon. Here they ate their mid-day meal.

All around them lay the ancient scenes of battle, murder and sudden death. Opposite was the dark bulk of Mount Gilboa, where

Gideon sifted out his chosen band to attack the host of Midian, and where desperate Saul killed himself with his own sword because he had lost a battle to the Philistines. Not far away the savage Jael drove her tent-pin through the temples of the sleeping Sisera. In Jezreel on a spur of Mount Gilboa, the painted hag, Queen Jezebel, looked from her palace window to see Captain Jehu, the killer of her son and other kings, driving boldly up the street. "Is it peace," she cried, "thou Zimri, thy master's murderer?" So Jehu called out to two or three of her servants, and they threw the raddled royal harridan down from the high window, and her blood splashed on the wall, and Jehu's horses trod her under foot. "Bury her decently," he said, "for she was a king's daughter."

Little thought our lowly travellers of these by-gone strifes and cruelties. Mary and Joseph belonged to another kingdom. She was chosen to be the mother of the Prince of Peace, and she was going on foot, very quietly, to Bethlehem, in order that the words of the angel and the prophet might be fulfilled. This obedient resolve made her firm and fearless. On this purpose her whole being was centered.

Through the green vale of Jezreel they passed easily, for the going was nearly level. But when they came beyond the spurs of Mount Gilboa on the south, there was an abrupt drop of three hundred feet, down which the trail went in steep zig-zags, so that Mary dared not ride, but must go carefully afoot. Before them on its high mound in the long Jordan Valley rose the old city of Bethshan, now called Scythopolis, a heathen town and fortress.

"Not there," said Mary. "We can not lodge there! The very ground on which the idolaters built their houses is unclean. The Gentiles carry the taint of the wickedness by which the serpent corrupted Eve. Only the Jewish people have been cleansed from it. I am very tired; but let us go on till we come to a village of our own folk. A cottage there is better than a palace among the pagans."

So they trudged on to Bethabara, a poor hamlet beside the murmuring fords of the river Jordan. Here they were received into a humble house with that open hospitality which was practiced among the Jews, and rested well until the morning.

The river was swollen by the rains. The fords were greatly deepened and the muddy water was foaming over them. But Mary rode on Thistles, with her feet tucked up, and Joseph waded the stream below, with his strong left arm around her and his sturdy body pressing up against the little shivering beast to keep him from being swept down by the swift current.

On the eastern side the descent of the Jordan Valley was not hard, though the road was miry, for the rain fell in sheets, and Mary was thankful for the big goat's-hair cloak. All day long they journeyed, but night fell before they could reach the village of Succoth, where they had hoped to find lodging. So they camped on a rising ground above the deep trench in which the Jordan raged through its matted jungle towards the Dead Sea. The night was not very cold, for they were below the level of the Mediterranean; and though a few drops of rain were falling, still the air of the Ghor was soft and humid.

Mary was a poet by nature. In her heart the spring of song rose constant and flowed clear. Before she slept, she sang again that lyric she had made more than six months ago when she visited her cousin Elizabeth beside the crystal fount of Ain Karim:

> My soul doth magnify the Lord;
> My spirit hath rejoiced in God my Savior,
> For he hath regarded the low estate of his handmaid;
> Hereafter all the generations shall call me blessed.

The next day was heavier and more oppressive. The rain held off; but the path dropped steadily below the sea-level, eight hundred, nine hundred feet. These hill-people, accustomed to the pure light air of Galilee, found exertion more difficult.

But Mary's resolution did not fail. Step after step she plodded on. They passed Succoth, where Jacob had built him a house and made shelters for his cattle after his wrestling with the angel by the Brook Jabbok. That same little river was now pouring down in flood, and Joseph had to go a long way up and around before he could find a safe ford through its turbid, bluish waters.

Down the broadening Ghor the pilgrims held their way. There were few villages or human dwellings. On the evening of the third day, Mary's strength being almost spent, they were forced to camp again. This time they were nearer to the thick jungle of the river-bed, where savage beasts lurked—lions and leopards, jackals and wild boars. Joseph encircled the camp with a fire of thorn-bushes, which crackled and sent up sparks.

"They won't pass this," he said. "Don't be afraid, Mary."

"I'm afraid of nothing," she answered. "I will both lay me down in peace and sleep, for the Lord will watch over his Son whom I carry."

It was sprinkling rain, so she rolled herself in her big mantle and slept. But Joseph kept his fires going.

Once when the yapping of the jackals came nearer he heard also the fierce whine of a leopard, close to the fire, and saw a pair of green gleaming eyes in the darkness beyond. He hurled his heavy iron-pointed staff at them. There was a terrible cry of angry pain, a swift pattering of feet in the dark. Then silence. Mary slept on, for she was dead-tired.

The fourth day they reached Beth-Haran, very weary, and found a kindly shelter with poor folk. On the fifth morning they crossed the swollen ford with the aid of the villagers, passed around the stately city of Jericho with its palm-groves and rich gardens soaked in perpetual summer, and took the steep road south-west into the Judean hills.

Here the going was harder for Mary, heavy with child. Fleeting pains troubled her as she walked, and when she tried to ride it was worse. The Brook of Kedron, in summer a bare bed of stones, was now a foaming torrent. They got over it with difficulty. Poor Thistles trembled and slipped among the rocks. Once Mary would have been thrown into the water if Joseph had not caught her in his arms. She suffered more and more. But she was not to be conquered in her purpose.

At noon they rested and took food in a lonely gulch among the red rocks. Wearied by her pains, Mary fell into a brief, troubled sleep. A vision of sudden death came to her. She saw herself as a woman walking alone over a crimson plain, which rolled and tossed under her feet like a stormy sea. There was a roaring round about her as of many waters. Then the red ground split open and she sank down, down into death; but even as she sank, she lifted her child above her into safety. She woke with a little cry of pain. Joseph ran to comfort her.

"I am not afraid," she said. "I can go through the gates of death to bring forth my son and my Lord."

Towards nightfall they came over the last rugged hill into the little town of Bethlehem.

The inn was full, crowded with people who had come up to be registered; the courtyard swarmed with men and animals in noisy confusion; there was not a single vacant place in the alcoves which opened around it.

But Elizabeth, Mary's cousin, the wife of Zacharias the priest, was there to welcome them. Being forewarned by the letter from Mary that they were coming, she had climbed on foot ten miles across the hills from Bethcar where she lived, carrying her six-month-old son John, to meet the travellers from Nazareth.

She was gray-haired, over fifty years old, but a strong and hearty woman. She remembered well the day when young Mary had come to visit her in Bethcar more than six months ago, and the child within her had leaped in greeting to the mother of his coming Lord. That unconscious prophecy was now very near to its fulfillment. Elizabeth was a woman of experience, and she knew.

"Come with me," she said. "Come quickly, beloved! I have a place for you. It is a dry grotto in the face of the cliff behind the inn. It has been used as a stable. It has two stalls. In the further part there is nothing but an old ox; the other part is empty and clean, and there is plenty of dry straw for a bed, and there is also a clean manger for a cradle. It is all ready, come quickly!"

Elizabeth took command like a general. Mary clung to her, weeping half in pain and half in joy. Joseph followed, leading Thistles. The weary old ass was put into the stall with the ox. Elizabeth spread the straw for Mary's bed, with a deft hand. The baby John was sound asleep in another corner. Joseph looked in and went away, closing the rough wooden door behind him. Elizabeth was left alone with Mary, whose days were fulfilled that she should now bring forth the Saviour in Bethlehem of Judea.

Curtains of Holy Night

Part not the curtains of the night, friend of my soul. They are the wings of mystery brooding over the hidden things of life. They are the reserve of the Eternal.

Within that darkness are the sharpest pains and the deepest joys that mortal flesh can feel — interwoven griefs and gladness of spirit that words can never tell — fears and hopes so sacred that they should be kept secret save from God, who knoweth all.

If you part the curtains, these things are changed; they vanish into thin air. If you try to tell all, you lose part.

All things are lawful to speak of, but all things are not expedient. Reality is precious, but in the deepest depth of reality there is a mystery beyond utterance. Silence and shade lie round about it to guard it from profanation.

We like a man who tells the truth, and nothing but the truth. But the whole truth is more than man can tell.

How a life leaves this world we know not, except that the heart of flesh left behind ceases to beat. How a life enters this world we know not, except that the heart nourished by the mother's heart begins its own beating.

Let the curtains fall.

Leave the wise Elizabeth and her own sleeping babe, alone with the pure Mary and her son Jesus coming into the world to save sinners.

It is Holy Night.

Joy Cometh in the Morning

In the gray light before sunrise, Elizabeth talked with Mary, who was watching her baby asleep in the manger. Joseph was listening, silent and content.

"He is a splendid boy," said Elizabeth.

"Yes," said Mary.

But not quite so big and strong as my baby John was," said Elizabeth.

"No?" said Mary.

"Yet he will be greater than my John," said Elizabeth. "There is a look of heaven on his face, as if he came from there."

"Yes," said Mary.

"What are you going to call him?" asked Elizabeth. "He surely must have a noble Jewish name."

"His name is Jesus," spoke up Joseph. "The angel I saw in my dream told me that long ago. For it is he that shall save his people from their sins."

"Yes," said Mary.

At this moment steps and voices were heard outside. There was a soft knocking on the door. Joseph opened it. Four men were standing there. They were simple peasants with sun-burned faces and rough clothes, but their manners were gentle. The eldest spoke for the others.

"Sir," he said, "we are the shepherds of the sheep which are kept near-by for the Temple sacrifices. Our names are Zadok, Jotham, Shama, and Nathan; poor men, sir, but honest and well-known in the neighbourhood. We were watching our flocks last night by the towers of Migdal Eder, where one of the prophets foretold that the Messiah should first be made known. A wonderful strange thing happened to us there. May we come in and tell it — that is, if perchance there is a new-born child here, wrapped in swaddling-bands and lying in a manger?"

"He is here," said Joseph. Then after a glance at Elizabeth, who smiled, he added, "Come in, shepherds, but speak softly."

They entered, stepping as lightly as they could, and looked with wonder on the young child in his quaint bed. Kneeling, they told of their vision of the first angel, with his glad tidings that the Messiah was born in the city of David, and then of the flock of many angels singing glory to God, peace on earth, good will among men. The child John looked at the shepherds with wide eyes. The baby Jesus slept. Joseph and Elizabeth were amazed at the tale of the shepherds. But Mary, still and happy, kept all these sayings, pondering them in her heart. That is a mother's way.

When the shepherds had gone, Elizabeth rose up and nursed her own child. Then she made ready to go out.

"You must have a better lodging than this," she said. "It will be days and days before you can travel. I have two cousins here who have good houses. Their guest chambers were full last night because of the crowd in Bethlehem. But to-day one of them will surely have room for you. I will go and see."

While she was away, there came another stranger to the grotto— a young shepherd, a wanderer in ragged clothes, with a worn and weary face of many troubles. He also desired to see the mother and the wondrous babe of whom his fellows had told him. Of this visit and of its ending the record is written in the story of "The Sad Shepherd." Perhaps there were also other visitors.

Elizabeth came back before noon, with joy in her face.

"Lemuel-bar-Zillai is making his guest-room ready. Come, let us go quickly. He will be glad to entertain us."

The house was a little larger than their own in Nazareth. Master and mistress were happy to receive them with the ancient Jewish kindness; for they were not mere strangers, they were kinsfolk. Three days later the good Elizabeth, remembering that her husband was lonely in Bethcar, tramped over the hills again to her home beside the beautiful flowing fountain of Ain Karim. Joseph and Mary with the

young child Jesus stayed on in the house of Lemuel, welcome guests
—welcome as angels.

Old Rites with New Meaning

There were certain forms and ceremonies they had to observe according to the Jewish law. First of all, after eight days, there was the formal naming of the child and his sealing as a son of Israel by the rite handed down from the times of Abraham. Then, after thirty-one days more, Joseph and Mary must go up to the temple at Jerusalem, for the purification of the mother and her first-born son.

It was not a long journey—only five miles—and it was a happy one. They were poor, but they had money enough for the offering of the humble—a pair of turtle-doves or two young pigeons. So Mary dropped her coins into the third of the trumpet-shaped openings of the treasure chests which stood in the Court of the Women. The pair of doves was offered and the priest declared that the ransom of the first-born was paid.

An old praying man named Simeon, who frequented the Temple, and an ancient prophetess named Anna, a widow who spent all her time there, saw the infant Jesus with his parents and something told them that the Messiah for whom they had long waited had come at last.

> Now lettest thou thy servant depart, Lord,
> According to thy word, in peace—

quavered Simeon, holding the infant in his arms. Anna gave thanks to God, in her thin cracked voice, and spoke of the child to all her friends.

On their joyful way back to Bethlehem, Joseph and Mary passed the tomb of Rachel with its low white dome standing beside the road. A dim foreboding sorrow came over Mary's mind. She recalled the words of old Simeon in the Temple, about the sword which was to pierce through her own soul.

"I remember," she said, "there is a word in one of the prophets concerning Rachel; something about 'a voice heard in a high place, mourning and lamenting, Rachel weeping for her children because they are not.' Can this be an omen of grief for us and death for our Jesus? He is so little, and the world is so big and blind and cruel. He may perish in its ignorant crush."

"We must take good care of him, that is all," said Joseph. "He has been trusted to us. He cannot perish until his great task is done. God has promised. We are all in God's hand. We do not know how it will be worked out. We must do our part."

Visitors from Afar

The very next day there was a strange event which brought great cheer to the anxious parents, and amazement to the neighbours in Bethlehem. Down the narrow street swayed three tall, richly harnessed camels carrying three strangers in costly raiment. They halted in front of the house of Lemuel and dismounted.

They were wise men of the East, Magians from the mountains of Persia. They said that a sign in the sky had led them to do homage to a heavenly King whose coming was foretold by the book of Zoroaster, as well as by the Jewish prophets. So they let down their corded bales and brought out gifts of gold and frankincense and myrrh. Kneeling in the house, they presented their tribute to the child Jesus.

Then they returned to the country from which they came; not by way of Jerusalem, for a dream had warned them against going back to the fierce and suspicious King Herod; but by the same road which Joseph and Mary had travelled — past Jericho and up the Jordan Valley towards Babylon and the Persian highlands.

Whether the infant Jesus knew anything of this visit of the Magi, except perhaps the glitter of their gold and the sweet smell of their incense, who can tell? But doubtless his parents spoke to him about it in later years.

It was Mary's habit to hold things in memory and ponder their meaning. What might not this coming of the disciples of Zoroaster, princes from a far land, mean for her son Jesus? Was he indeed to be a light for revelation to the Gentiles, as well as the glory of his people in Israel?

Mary, devout and strict Jewess that she was, could hardly understand this idea. Yet because she was of a generous nature and loved giving, the thought entered her heart and stayed there. So it was mingled with the very food of life which her son drew from her breasts.

Home Again to Nazareth

Never in his life had Joseph the carpenter been so well-off for money as he was after the visit of the Wise Men. It was not vast wealth that they brought him, but it was enough to make him easy in mind and hopeful for the future.

First, there were the rare and precious gums of frankincense and myrrh, the surplus of which could be sold for a considerable sum. Second, there was the gold, not a huge quantity, but at least a tribute worthy to be presented by princes to the Prince. With this small capital in hand, Joseph could easily reward Lemuel for the generous entertainment he had provided, and perhaps set himself up in his trade and stay on as a carpenter in Bethlehem.

The idea appealed to him strongly, for Bethlehem was a pleasant place in a fertile region. He had made friends there, and it was near the Temple. Lemuel favoured the plan.

"There are two carpenters here already," said he, "but there is room and need for another. The town is growing. We are right on the road from Jerusalem to Egypt, where the caravans pass. They give a lot of work in repairs on pack-saddles and chariots. I know of a good place for a work-shop. You will do well to stay here."

"I think so, too," said Joseph. "There will be plenty for me to do. And though the pleasure-palace of that vile fox Herod is on the mountain top just before us, and Jerusalem is full of heathen, after all it is the center of Israel, the holy city where the true King must be lifted up and crowned."

While the two men were busy talking, Mary was silent. She was thinking of the dear, gray little house in Nazareth, the silvery olive-trees in the small garden, the flowing spring under its stone arch, the friendly peace of the hills and vales of Galilee.

Did not the old rabbis say that Galilee was a better place than Judea to bring up a child? Was not that her first and dearest duty, the holy charge given to her hands? Yet of course she would do what her husband wanted; stay with him here in Bethlehem, or go with him anywhere in the wide world.

Joseph slept at noon that day, and another dream came to him — a strange, sudden dream, disquieting, full of alarm. They were great dreamers in those times, and they paid attention to their visions.

This new dream was terrifying.

An angel told of Herod's crazy design to have all the infant boys in Bethlehem killed by his soldiers, hoping thus to destroy the young child whom he feared and hated as his predicted rival for the throne. It was a madman's idea, unspeakably cruel. But what was that to a crafty lunatic who had already killed his wife, his mother-in-law, his uncle, and his own sons, Alexander, Aristobulus, and Antipater? The Jews knew Herod too well to doubt his readiness for any bloody villainy. Joseph was numb with the terror of the dream.

"Get up," said the angel, "and take the young child and his mother, and flee into Egypt, and stay there until I tell thee."

So Joseph rose quickly, and told Mary and their kind hosts the strange message that had come to him.

With part of his gold he bought a strong white ass of the famous breed of the Nile, and plenty of gear for the journey. Hasty were the preparations and the farewells.

Dark was the night when the holy family took the great south road for the distant land of the Sphinx and the Pyramids, the land where the children of Israel were once in bondage and where the ancient idols still throned in their crumbling temples.

The young child who was born to overthrow them had no throne but his mother's breast. There he reigned, in peace and joy, while the strong ass bore them through the darkness towards the exile and safety.

It was the longest journey that Jesus ever took on earth.

What befell them in Egypt, and what they saw there, we do not know and can not guess.

What is certain is that the holy family stayed there until the wicked Herod died of a loathsome disease, and his son Archelaus reigned in his stead over Judea. Then Joseph made up his mind that it would be safe to go back to Judea and set up that new carpenter-shop which he had planned with his friend Lemuel.

But it was not to be so. Another dream came to him in which he was warned not to return to Bethlehem, but to go straight on to his old home in Galilee.

So Mary came again to the little gray house that she loved and the carpenter-shop in Nazareth.

There it was that the thought of Jesus had first entered Mary's heart.

So there it was that the boy lived, and was obedient to his parents and grew strong, filled with wisdom. The grace of God was upon him; and in due time he came forth from that little hill-town on his great mission to serve and save the world.

The Birth of Jesus

he birth of Jesus is the sunrise of the Bible. Towards this point the aspirations of the prophets and the poems of the psalmists were directed as the heads of flowers are turned toward the dawn. From this point a new day began to flow very silently over the world—a day of faith and freedom, a day of hope and love. When we remember the high meaning that has come into human life and the clear light that has flooded softly down from the manger-cradle in Bethlehem of Judea, we do not wonder that mankind has learned to reckon history from the birthday of Jesus, and to date all events by the years before or after the Nativity of Christ.

The Lost Word

ome down, Hermas, come down! The night is past. It is time to be stirring. Christ is born today. Peace be with you in His name. Make haste and come down!"

A little group of young men were standing in a street of Antioch, in the dusk of early morning, fifteen hundred years ago—a class of candidates who had nearly finished their years of training for the Christian church. They had come to call their fellow-student Hermas from his lodging.

Their voices rang out cheerily through the cool air. They were full of that glad sense of life which the young feel when they have risen early and come to rouse one who is still sleeping. There was a note of friendly triumph in their call, as if they were exulting unconsciously in having begun the adventure of the new day before their comrade.

But Hermas was not asleep. He had been waking for hours, and the walls of his narrow lodging had been a prison to his heart. A nameless sorrow and discontent had fallen upon him, and he could find no escape from the heaviness of his own thoughts.

There is a sadness of youth into which the old cannot enter. It seems unreal and causeless. But it is even more bitter and burdensome than the sadness of age. There is a sting of resentment in it, a fever of angry surprise that the world should so soon be a disappointment, and life so early take on the look of a failure. It has little reason in it, perhaps, but it has all the more weariness and gloom, because the man who is oppressed by it feels dimly that it is an unnatural thing that he should be tired of living before he has fairly begun to live.

Hermas had fallen into the very depths of this strange self-pity. He was out of tune with everything around him. He had been thinking, through the dead night, of all that he had given up when he left the house of his father, the wealthy pagan Demetrius, to join the company of the Christians. Only two years ago he had been one of the richest young men in Antioch. Now he was one of the poorest. The worst of it was that, though he had made the choice willingly and with a kind of enthusiasm, he was already dissatisfied with it.

The new life was no happier than the old. He was weary of vigils and fasts, weary of studies and penances, weary of prayers and sermons. He felt like a slave in a treadmill. He knew that he must go on. His honour, his conscience, his sense of duty, bound him. He could not go back to the old careless pagan life again; for something had happened within him which made a return impossible. Doubtless he had found the true religion, but he had found it only as a task and a burden; its joy and peace had sliped away from him.

He felt disillusioned and robbed. He sat beside his hard couch, waiting without expectancy for the gray dawn of another empty day, and hardly lifting his head at the shouts of his friends.

"Come down, Hermas, you sluggard! Come down! It is Christmas morn. Awake, and be glad with us!"

"I am coming," he answered listlessly. "Only have patience a moment. I have been awake since midnight, and waiting for the day."

"You hear him!" said his friends one to another. "How he puts us all to shame! He is more watchful, more eager, than any of us. Our master, John the Presbyter, does well to be proud of him. He is the best man in our class."

While they were talking the door opened and Hermas stepped out. He was a figure to be remarked in any company—tall, broad-shouldered, straight-hipped, with a head proudly poised on the firm column of the neck, and short brown curls clustering over the square forehead. It was the perpetual type of vigorous and intelligent young manhood, such as may be found in every century among the throngs of ordinary men, as if to show what the flower of the race should be. But the light in his eyes was clouded and uncertain; his smooth cheeks were leaner than they should have been at twenty; and there were downward lines about his mouth which spoke of desires unsatisfied and ambitions repressed. He joined his companions with brief greetings—a nod to one, a word to another—and they passed together down the steep street.

Overhead the mystery of daybreak was silently transfiguring the sky. The curtain of darkness had lifted along the edge of the horizon. The ragged crests of Mount Silpius were outlined with pale saffron light. In the central vault of heaven a few large stars twinkled drowsily. The great city, still chiefly pagan, lay more than half-asleep. But multitudes of the Christians, dressed in white and carrying lighted torches in their hands, were hurrying toward the Basilica of Constantine to keep the new holy-day of the church, the festival of the birthday of their Master.

The vast, bare building was soon crowded, and the younger converts, who were not yet permitted to stand among the baptized, found it difficult to come to their appointed place between the first two pillars of the house, just within the threshold. There was some good-humoured pressing and jostling about the door; but the candidates pushed steadily forward.

"By your leave, friends, our station is beyond you. Will you let us pass? Many thanks."

A touch here, a courteous nod there, a little patience, a little persistence, and at last they stood in their place. Hermas was taller than his companions; he could look easily over their heads and survey the sea of people stretching away through the columns, under the shadows of the high roof, as the tide spreads on a calm day into the pillared cavern of Staffa, quiet as if the ocean hardly dared to breathe. The light of many torches fell, in flickering, uncertain rays, over the assembly. At the end of the vista there was a circle of clearer, steadier radiance. Hermas could see the bishop in his great chair, surrounded by the presbyters, the lofty desks on either side for the readers of the Scripture, the communion-table and the table of offerings in the middle of the church.

The call to prayer sounded down the long aisle. Thousands of hands were joyously lifted in the air, as if the sea had blossomed into waving lilies, and the "Amen" was like the murmur of countless ripples in an echoing place.

Then the singing began, led by the choir of a hundred trained voices which the Bishop Paul had founded in Antioch. Timidly, at first, the music felt its way, as the people joined with a broken and uncertain cadence: the mingling of many little waves not yet gathered into rhythm and harmony. Soon the longer, stronger billows of song rolled in, sweeping from side to side as the men and the women answered in the clear antiphony.

Hermas had often been carried on those tides of music's golden sea setting toward eternity.

But to-day his heart was a rock that stood motionless. The flood passed by and left him unmoved.

Looking out from his place at the foot of the pillar, he saw a man standing far off in the lofty bema. Short and slender, wasted by sickness, gray before his time, with pale cheeks and wrinkled brow, he seemed at first like a person of no significance—a reed shaken in the wind. But there was a look in his deep-set, poignant eyes, as he gathered all the glances of the multitude to himself, that belied his mean appearance and prophesied power. Hermas knew very well who it was: the man who had drawn him from his father's house, the teacher who was instructing him as a son in the Christian faith, the guide and trainer of his soul—John of Antioch, whose fame filled the city and began to overflow Asia, and who was called already Chrysostom, the golden-mouthed preacher.

Hermas had felt the magic of his eloquence many a time; and to-day, as the tense voice vibrated through the stillness, and the sentences moved onward, growing fuller and stronger, bearing precious cargo of costly rhetoric and treasures of homely speech in their bosom, and drawing the hearts of men with a resistless magic, Hermas knew that the preacher had never been more potent, more inspired.

He played on that immense congregation as a master on an instrument. He rebuked their sins, and they trembled. He touched their sorrows, and they wept. He spoke of the conflicts, the triumphs, the glories of their faith, and they broke out in thunders of applause. He hushed them into reverent silence, and led them tenderly, with the wise men of the East, to the lowly birthplace of Jesus.

"Do thou, therefore, likewise leave the Jewish people, the troubled city, the bloodthirsty tyrant, the pomp of the world, and hasten to Bethlehem, the sweet house of spiritual bread. For though thou be but a shepherd, and come hither, thou shalt behold the young Child in an inn. Though thou be a king, and come not hither, thy purple robe shall profit thee nothing. Though thou be one of the wise men, this shall be no hindrance to thee. Only let thy coming be to honour and adore, with trembling joy, the Son of God, to whose name be glory, on this His birthday, and forever and forever."

The soul of Hermas did not answer to the musician's touch. The strings of his hearts were slack and soundless; there was no response within him. He was neither shepherd, nor king, nor wise man; only an unhappy, dissatisfied, questioning youth. He was out of sympathy with the eager preacher, the joyous hearers. In their harmony he had no part. Was it for this that he had forsaken his inheritance and narrowed his life to poverty and hardship? What was it all worth?

The gracious prayers with which the young converts were blessed and dismissed before the sacrament sounded hollow in his ears. Never had he felt so utterly lonely as in that praying throng. He went out with his companions like a man departing from a banquet where all but he had been fed.

"Farewell, Hermas," they cried, as he turned from them at the door. But he did not look back, nor wave his hand. He was already alone in his heart.

When he entered the broad Avenue of the Colonnades, the sun had already topped the eastern hills, and the ruddy light was streaming through the long double row of archways and over the pavements of crimson marble. But Hermas turned his back to the morning, and walked with his shadow before him.

The street began to swarm and whirl and quiver with the motley life of a huge city: beggars and jugglers, dancers and musicians, gilded youths in their chariots, and daughters of joy looking out from their windows, all intoxicated with the mere delight of living and the gladness of a new day. The pagan populace of Antioch—reckless, pleasure-loving, spendthrift—were preparing for the Saturnalia. But all this Hermas had renounced. He cleft his way through the crowd slowly, like a reluctant swimmer weary of breasting the tide.

At the corner of the street where the narrow, populous Lane of the Camel-drivers crossed the Colonnades, a story-teller had bewitched a circle of people around him. It was the same old tale of love and adventure that many generations have listened to; but the lively fancy of the hearers lent in new interest, and the wit of the improviser drew forth sighs of interest and shouts of laughter.

A yellow-haired girl on the edge of the throng turned, as Hermas passed, and smiled in his face. She put out her hand and caught him by the sleeve.

"Stay," she said, "and laugh a bit with us. I know who you are—the son of Demetrius. You must have bags of gold. Why do you look so black? Love is alive yet."

Hermas shook off her hand, but not ungently.

"I don't know what you mean," he said. "You are mistaken in me. I am poorer than you are."

But as he passed on, he felt the warm touch of her fingers through the cloth on his arm. It seemed as if she had plucked him by the heart.

He went out by the Western Gate, under the golden cherubim that the Emperor Titus had stolen from the ruined Temple of Jerusalem and fixed upon the arch of triumph. He turned to the left, and climbed the hill to the road that led to the Grove of Daphne.

In all the world there was no other highway as beautiful. It wound for five miles along the foot of the mountains, among gardens and villas, plantations of myrtles and mulberries, with wide outlooks over the valley of Orontes and the distant, shimmering sea.

The richest of all the dwellings was the House of the Golden Pillars, the mansion of Demetrius. He had won the favor of the apostate Emperor Julian, whose vain efforts to restore the worship of the heathen gods, some twenty years ago, had opened an easy way to wealth and power for all who would mock and oppose Christianity. Demetrius was not a sincere fanatic like his royal master; but he was bitter enough in his professed scorn of the new religion, to make him a favourite at the court where the old religion was in fashion. He had reaped a rich reward of his policy, and a strange sense of consistency made him more fiercely loyal to it than if it had been a real faith. He was proud of being called "the friend of Julian"; and when his son joined himself to the Christians, and acknowledged the unseen God, it seemed like an insult to his father's success. He drove the boy from his door and disinherited him.

The glittering portico of the serene, haughty house, the repose of the well-ordered garden, still blooming with belated flowers, seemed at once to deride and to invite the young outcast plodding along the dusty road. "This is your birthright," whispered the clambering rose-trees by the gate; and the closed portals of carven bronze said: "You have sold it for a thought—a dream."

Hermas found the Grove of Daphne quite deserted. There was no sound in the enchanted vale but the rustling of the light winds chasing each other through the laurel thickets, and the babble of innumerable streams. Memories of the days and nights of delicate pleasure that the grove had often seen still haunted the bewildered paths and broken fountains. At the foot of a rocky hill, crowned with the ruins of Apollo's temple, which had been mysteriously destroyed by fire just after Julian had restored and reconsecrated it, Hermas sat down beside a gushing spring, and gave himself up to sadness.

"How beautiful the world would be, how joyful, how easy to live in, without religion! These questions about unseen things, perhaps about unreal things, these restraints and duties and sacrifices—if I were only free from them all, and could only forget them all, then I could live my life as I pleased, and be happy."

"Why not?" said a quiet voice at his back.

He turned, and saw an old man with a long beard and a threadbare cloak (the garb affected by the pagan philosophers) standing behind him and smiling curiously.

"How is it that you answer that which has not been spoken?" said Hermas. "And who are you that honor me with your company?"

"Forgive the intrusion," answered the stranger. "It is not ill meant. A friendly interest is as good as an introduction."

"But to what singular circumstance do I owe this interest?"

"To your face," said the old man, with a courteous inclination. "Perhaps also a little to the fact that I am the oldest inhabitant here, and feel as if all visitors were my guests, in a way."

"Are you, then, one of the keepers of the grove? And have you given up your work with the trees to take a holiday as a philosopher?"

"Not at all. The robe of philosophy is a mere affectation, I must confess. I think little of it. My profession is the care of altars. In fact, I am the solitary priest of Apollo whom the Emperor Julian found here when he came to revive the worship of the grove, some twenty years ago. You have heard of the incident?"

"Yes," said Hermas, beginning to be interested. "The whole city must have heard of it, for it is still talked of. But surely it was a strange sacrifice that you brought to celebrate the restoration of Apollo's temple?"

"You mean the ancient goose?" said the old man laughing. "Well, perhaps it was not precisely what the emperor expected. But it was all that I had, and it seemed to me not inappropriate. You will agree to that if you are a Christian, as I guess from your dress."

"You speak lightly for a priest of Apollo."

"Oh, as for that, I am no bigot. The priesthood is a professional matter, and the name of Apollo is as good as any other. How many altars do you think there have been in this grove?"

"I do not know."

"Just four-and-twenty, including that of the martyr Babylas, whose ruined chapel you see just beyond us. I have had something to do with most of them in my time. They are transitory. They give employment to care-takers for a while. But the thing that lasts, and the thing that interests me, is the human life that plays around them. The game has been going on for centuries. It still disports itself very pleasantly on summer evenings through these shady walks. Believe me, for I know. Daphne and Apollo are shadows. But the flying maidens and the pursuing lovers, the music and the dances, these are realities. Life is a game, and the world keeps it up merrily. But you? You are of a sad countenance for one so young and so fair. Are you a loser in the game?"

The words and tone of the speaker fitted Hermas' mood as a key fits the lock. He opened his heart to the old man, and told him the story of his life: his luxurious boyhood in his father's house; the irresistible spell which compelled him to forsake it when he heard John's preaching of the new religion; his lonely year with the Anchorites among the mountains; the strict discipline in his teacher's house at Antioch; his weariness of duty, his distaste for poverty, his discontent with worship.

"And to-day," said he, "I have been thinking that I am a fool. My life is swept as bare as a hermit's cell. There is nothing in it but a dream, a thought of God, which does not satisfy me."

The singular smile deepened on his companion's face. "You are ready, then," he suggested, "to renounce your religion and go back to that of your father?"

"No; I renounce nothing. I accept nothing. I do not wish to think about it. I only wish to live."

"A very reasonable wish, and I think you are about to see its accomplishment. Indeed, I may even say that I can put you in the way of securing it. Do you believe in magic?"

"I do not know whether I believe in anything. This is not a day on which I care to make professions of faith. I believe in what I see. I want what will give me pleasure."

"Well," said the old man, soothingly, as he plucked a leaf from the laurel-tree above them and dipped it in the spring, "let us dimiss the riddles of belief. I like them as little as you do. You know this is a Castalian fountain. The Emperor Hadrian once read his fortune here from a leaf dipped in the water. Let us see what this leaf tells us. It is already turning yellow. How do you read that?"

"Wealth," said Hermas, laughing, as he looked at his mean garments.

"And here is a bud on the stem that seems to be swelling. What is that?"

"Pleasure," answered Hermas, bitterly.

"And here is a tracing of wreaths upon the surface. What do you make of that?"

"What you will," said Hermas, not even taking the trouble to look. "Suppose we say success and fame?"

"Yes," said the stranger. "It is all written here. I promise that you shall enjoy it all. But you do not need to believe in my promise. I am not in the habit of requiring faith of those whom I would serve. No such hard conditions for me! There is only one thing that I ask. This is the season that you Christians call the Christmas, and you have taken up the pagan custom of exchanging gifts. Well, if I give to you, you must give to me. It is a small thing, and really the thing you can best afford to part with: a single word—the name of Him you profess to worship. Let me take that word and all that belongs to it entirely out of your life, so that you shall never hear it or speak it again. You will be richer without it. I promise you everything, and this is all I ask in return. Do you consent?"

"Yes. I consent," said Hermas, mocking. "If you can take your price, a word, you can keep your promise, a dream."

The stranger laid the long, cool, wet leaf softly across the young man's eyes. An icicle of pain darted through them; every nerve in his body was drawn together there in a knot of agony.

Then all the tangle of pain seemed to be lifted out of him. A cool languor of delight flowed back through every vein, and he sank into a profound sleep.

There is a slumber so deep that it annihilates time. It is like a fragment of eternity. Beneath its enchantment of vacancy, a day seems like a thousand years, and a thousand years might well pass as one day.

It was such a sleep that fell upon Hermas in the Grove of Daphne. An immeasurable period, an interval of life so blank and empty that he could not tell whether it was long or short, had passed over him when his senses began to stir again. The setting sun was shooting arrows of gold under the glossy laurel-leaves. He rose and stretched his arms, grasping a smooth branch above him and shaking it, to be sure that he was alive. Then he hurried back toward Antioch, treading lightly as if on air.

The ground seemed to spring beneath his feet. Already his life had changed, he knew not how. Something that did not belong to him had dropped away; he had returned to a former state of being.

He felt as if anything might happen to him, and he was ready for anything. He was a new man, yet curiously familiar to himself—as if he had done with playing a tiresome part and returned to his natural state. He was buoyant and free, without a care, a doubt, a fear.

As he drew near to his father's house he saw a confusion of servants in the porch, and the old steward ran down to meet him at the gate.

"Lord, we have been seeking you everywhere. The master is at the point of death, and has sent for you. Since the sixth hour he calls your name continually. Come to him quickly, lord, for I fear the time is short."

Hermas entered the house at once; nothing could amaze him to-day. His father lay on an ivory couch in the inmost chamber, with shrunken face and restless eyes, his lean fingers picking incessantly at the silken coverlet.

"My son!" he murmured. "Hermas, my son! It is good that you have come back to me. I have missed you. I was wrong to send you away. You shall never leave me again. You are my son, my heir. I have changed everything. Hermas, my son, come nearer—close beside me. Take my hand, my son!"

The young man obeyed, and, kneeling by the couch, gathered his father's cold, twitching fingers in his firm, warm grasp.

"Hermas, life is passing—long, rich, prosperous; the last sands, I cannot stay them. My religion, a good policy—Julian was my friend. But now he is gone—where? My soul is empty—nothing beyond— very dark—I am afraid. But you know something better. You found something that made you willing to give up your life for it—it must have been almost like dying—yet you were happy. What was it you found? See, I am giving you everything. I have forgiven you. Now forgive me. Tell, me, what is it? Your secret, your faith—give it to me before I go."

At the sound of this broken pleading a strange passion of pity and love took the young man by the throat. His voice shook a little as he answered eagerly, "Father, there is nothing to forgive. I am your son; I will gladly tell you all that I know. I will give you the secret. Father, you must believe with all your heart, and soul, and strength, in—"

Where was the word—the word that he had been used to utter night and morning, the word that had meant to him more than he had ever known? What had become of it?

He groped for it in the dark room of his mind. He had thought he could lay his hand upon it in a moment, but it was gone. Some one had taken it away. Everything else was most clear to him: the terror of death; the lonely soul appealing from his father's eyes; the instant need of comfort and help. But at the one point where he looked for help he could find nothing; only an empty space. The word of hope had vanished. He felt for it blindly and in desperate haste.

"Father, wait! I have forgotten something—it has slipped away from me. I shall find it in a moment. There is hope—I will tell you presently—oh, wait!"

The bony hand gripped his like a vise; the glazed eyes opened wider. "Tell me," whispered the old man. "Tell me quickly, for I must go."

The voice sank like a dull rattle. The fingers closed once more, and relaxed. The light behind the eyes went out.

Hermas, the master of the House of the Golden Pillars, was keeping watch by the dead.

The break with the old life was as clean as if it had been cut with a knife. Some faint image of a hermit's cell, a bare lodging in a back street of Antioch, a class-room full of earnest students, remained in Hermas' memory. Some dull echo of the voice of John the Presbyter, and the measured sound of chanting, and the murmur of great congregations, still lingered in his ears; but it was like something that had happened to another person, something that he had read long ago, but of which he had lost the meaning.

His new life was full and smooth and rich—too rich for any sense of loss to make itself felt. There were a hundred affairs to busy him, and the days ran swiftly by as if they were shod with winged sandals.

Nothing needed to be considered, prepared for, begun. Everything was ready and waiting for him. All that he had to do was to go on.

The estate of Demetrius was even greater than the world had supposed. There were fertile lands in Syria which the emperor had given him, marble-quarries in Phrygia, and forests of valuable timber in Cilicia; the vaults of the villa contained chests of gold and silver; the secret cabinets in the master's room were full of precious stones. The stewards were diligent and faithful. The servants of the household rejoiced at the young master's return. His table was spread; the rose-garland of pleasure was woven for his head; his cup was overflowing with the spicy wine of power.

The period of mourning for his father came at a fortunate moment to seclude and safeguard him from the storm of political troubles and persecutions that fell upon Antioch after the insults offered by the people to the imperial statues in the year 387. The friends of Demetrius, prudent and conservative persons, gathered around Hermas and made him welcome to their circle. Chief among them was Libanius, the sophist, his nearest neighbour, whose daughter Athenais had been the playmate of Hermas in the old days.

He had left her a child. He found her a beautiful woman. What transformation is so magical, so charming, as this? To see the uncertain lines of youth rounded into firmness and symmetry, to discover the half-ripe, merry, changing face of the girl matured into perfect loveliness, and looking at you with calm, clear, serious eyes, not forgetting the past, but fully conscious of the changed present—this is to behold a miracle in the flesh.

"Where have you been, these two years?" asked Athenais, as they walked together through the garden of lilies where they had so often played.

"In a land of tiresome dreams," answered Hermas. "But you have wakened me, and I am never going back again."

It was not to be supposed that the sudden disappearance of Hermas from among his former associates could long remain unnoticed. At first it was a mystery. There was a fear, for two or three days, that he might be lost. Some of his more intimate companions maintained that his devotion had led him out into the desert to join the Anchorites. But the news of his return to the House of the Golden Pillars, and of his new life as its master, filtered quickly through the gossip of the city.

Then the church was filled with dismay and grief and reproach. Messengers and letters were sent to Hermas. They disturbed him a little, but they took no hold upon him. It seemed to him as if the messengers spoke in a strange language. As he read the letters there were words blotted out of the writing which made the full sense unintelligible.

His old companions came to reprove him for leaving them, to warn him of the peril of apostasy, to entreat him to return. It all sounded vague and futile. They spoke as if he had betrayed or offended some one; but when they came to name the object of his fear—the one whom he had displeased, and to whom he should return—he heard nothing;

there was a blur of silence in their speech. The clock pointed to the hour, but the bell did not strike. At last Hermas refused to see them any more.

One day John the Presbyter stood in the atrium. Hermas was entertaining Libanius and Athenais in the banquet-hall. When the visit of the Presbyter was announced, the young master loosed a collar of gold and jewels from his neck, and gave it to his scribe.

"Take this to John of Antioch, and tell him it is a gift from his former pupil—as a token of remembrance, or to spend for the poor of the city. I will always send him what he wants, but it is idle for us to talk together any more. I do not understand what he says. I have not gone to the temple, nor offered sacrifices, nor denied his teaching. I have simply forgotten. I do not think about those things any longer. I am only living. A happy man wishes him all happiness and farewell."

But John let the golden collar fall on the marble floor. "Tell your master that we shall talk together again, in due time," said he, as he passed sadly out of the hall.

The love of Athenais and Hermas was like a tiny rivulet that sinks out of sight in a cavern, but emerges again a bright and brimming stream. The careless camradery of childhood was mysteriously changed into a complete companionship.

When Athenais entered the House of the Golden Pillars as a bride, all the music of life came with her. Hermas called the feast of her welcome "the banquet of the full chord." Day after day, night after night, week after week, month after month, the bliss of the home unfolded like a rose of a thousand leaves. When a child came to them, a strong, beautiful boy, worthy to be the heir of such a house, the heart of the rose was filled with overflowing fragrance. Happiness was heaped upon happiness. Every wish brought its own accomplishment. Wealth, honor, beauty, peace, love—it was an abundance of felicity so great that the soul of Hermas could hardly contain it.

Strangely enough, it began to press upon him, to trouble him with the very excess of joy. He felt as if there were something yet needed to complete and secure it all. There was an urgency within him, a longing to find some outlet for his feelings, he knew not how—some expression and culmination of his happiness, he knew not what.

Under his joyous demeanour a secret fire of restlessness began to burn—an expectancy of something yet to come which should put the touch of perfection on his life. He spoke of it to Athenais, as they sat together, one summer evening, in a bower of jasmine, with their boy playing at their feet. There had been music in the garden; but now the singers and lute-players had withdrawn, leaving the master and mistress alone in the lingering twilight, tremulous with inarticulate melody of unseen birds. There was a secret voice in the hour seeking vainly for utterance—a word waiting to be spoken.

"How deep is our happiness, my beloved!" said Hermas. "Deeper than the sea that slumbers yonder, below the city. And yet it is not quite full and perfect. There is a depth of joy that we have not yet known—a repose of happiness that is still beyond us. What is it? I have no superstitions, like the king who cast his signet-ring into the sea because he dreaded that some secret vengeance would fall on his unbroken good fortune. That was an idle terror. But there is something that oppresses me like an invisible burden. There is something still undone, unspoken, unfelt—something that we need to complete everything. Have you not felt it, too? Can you not lead me to it?"

"Yes," she answered, lifting her eyes to his face. "I, too, have felt it, Hermas, this burden, this need, this unsatisfied longing. I think I know what it means. It is gratitude—the language of the heart, the music of happiness. There is no perfect joy without gratitude. But we have never learned it, and the want of it troubles us. It is like being dumb with a heart full of love. We must find the word for it, and say it together. Then we shall be perfectly joined in perfect joy. Come, my dear lord, let us take the boy with us, and give thanks."

Hermas lifted the child in his arms, and turned with Athenais into the depth of the garden. There was a dismantled shrine of some forgotten fashion of worship half-hidden among the luxuriant flowers. A fallen image lay beside it, face downward in the grass. They stood there, hand in hand, the boy drowsily resting on his father's shoulder.

Silently the rose-colored light caressed the tall spires of the cypress-trees; silently the shadows gathered at their feet; silently the tranquil stars looked out from the deepening arch of heaven. The very breath of life itself paused. It was the hour of culmination, the supreme moment of felicity waiting for its crown. The tones of Hermas were clear and low as he began, half-speaking and half-chanting, in rhythm of an ancient song:

"Fair is the world, the sea, the sky, the double kingdom of day and night, in the glow of morning, in the shadow of evening, and under the dripping light of stars.

"Fairer still is life in our breasts, with its manifold music and meaning, with its wonder of seeing and hearing and feeling and knowing and being.

"Fairer and still more fair is love, that draws us together, mingles over lives in its flow, and bears them along like a river, strong and clear and swift, reflecting the stars in its bosom.

"Wide is our world; we are rich; we have all things. Life is abundant within us—a measureless deep. Deepest of all is our love, and it longs to speak.

"Come, thou final word! Come, thou crown of speech! Come, thou charm of peace! Open the gates of our hearts. Lift the weight of our joy and bear it upward.

"For all good gifts, for all perfect gifts, for love, for life, for the world, we praise, we bless, we thank—"

As a soaring bird, struck by an arrow, falls headlong from the sky, so the song of Hermas fell. At the end of his flight of gratitude there was nothing—a blank, a hollow space.

He looked for a face, and saw a void. He sought for a hand, and clasped vacancy. His heart was throbbing and swelling with passion; the bell swung to and fro within him, beating from side to side as if it would burst; but not a single note came from it. All the fullness of his feeling, that had risen upward like a fountain, fell back from the empty sky, as cold as snow, as hard as hail, frozen and dead. There was no meaning in his happiness. No one had sent it to him. There was no one to thank for it. His felicity was a closed circle, a wall of ice.

"Let us go back," he said sadly to Athenais. "The child is heavy upon my shoulder. We will lay him to sleep, and go into the library. The air grows chilly. We were mistaken. The gratitude of life is only a dream. There is no one to thank."

And in the garden it was already night.

No outward change came to the House of the Golden Pillars. Everything moved as smoothly, as delicately, as prosperously, as before. But inwardly there was a subtle, inexplicable transformation. A vague discontent, a final and inevitable sense of incompleteness, overshadowed the existence from that night when Hermas realized that his joy could never go beyond itself.

The next morning the old man whom he had seen in the Grove of Daphne, but never since, appeared mysteriously at the door of the house, as if he had been sent for, and entered like an invited guest.

Hermas could not but make him welcome, and at first he tried to regard him with reverence and affection as the one through whom fortune had come. But it was impossible. There was a chill in the inscrutable smile of Marcion, as he called himself, that seemed to mock at reverence. He was in the house as one watching a strange experiment—tranquil, interested, ready to supply anything that might be needed for its completion, but thoroughly indifferent to the feelings of the subject; an anatomist of life, looking curiously to see how long it would continue, and how it would act, after the heart had been removed.

In his presence Hermas was conscious of a certain irritation, a resentful anger against the calm, frigid scrutiny of the eyes that followed him everywhere, like a pair of spies, peering out over the smiling mouth and the long white beard.

"Why do you look at me so curiously?" asked Hermas, one morning, as they sat together in the library. "Do you see anything strange in me?"

"No," answered Marcion, "something familiar."

"And what is that?"

"A singular likeness to a discontented young man that I met some years ago in the Grove of Daphne."

"But why should that interest you? Surely it was to be expected."

"A thing that we expect often surprises us when we see it. Besides, my curiosity is piqued. I suspect you of keeping a secret from me."

"You are jesting with me. There is nothing in my life that you do not know. What is the secret?"

"Nothing more than the wish to have one. You are growing tired of your bargain. The play wearies you. That is foolish. Do you want to try a new part?"

The question was like a mirror upon which one comes suddenly in a half-lighted room. A quick illumination falls on it, and the passer-by is startled by the look of his own face.

"You are right," said Hermas. "I am tired. We have been going on stupidly in this house, as if nothing were possible but what my father had done before me. There is nothing original in being rich, and well-fed, and well-dressed. Thousands of men have tried it, and have not been satisfied. Let us do something new. Let us make a mark in the world."

"It is well said," nodded the old man. "You are speaking again like a man after my own heart. There is no folly but the loss of an opportunity to enjoy a new sensation."

From that day Hermas seemed to be possessed with a perpetual haste, an uneasiness that left him no repose. The summit of life had been attained, the highest possible point of felicity. Henceforward the course could only be at a level—perhaps downward. It might be brief; at the best it could not be very long. It was madness to lose a day, an hour. That would be the only fatal mistake: to forfeit anything of the bargain that he had made. He would have it, and hold it, and enjoy it all to the full. The world might have nothing better to give than it had already given; but surely it had many things that were new, and Marcion should help him to find them.

Under his learned counsel the House of the Golden Pillars took on a new magnificence. Artists were brought from Corinth and Rome and Alexandria to adorn it with splendour. Its fame glittered around the world. Banquets of incredible luxury drew the most celebrated guests into its dining area, and filled them with envious admiration. The bees swarmed and buzzed about the golden hive. The human insects, gorgeous moths of pleasure and greedy flies of appetite, parasites and flatterers and crowds of inquisitive idlers, danced and fluttered in the dazzling light that surrounded Hermas.

Everything that he touched prospered. He bought a tract of land in the Caucasus, and emeralds were discovered among the mountains.

He sent a fleet of wheat-ships to Italy, and the price of grain doubled while it was on the way. He sought political favor with the emperor, and was rewarded with the governorship of the city. His name was a word to conjure with.

The beauty of Athenais lost nothing with the passing seasons, but grew near perfect, even under the inexplicable shade of dissatisfaction that sometimes veiled it. "Fair as the wife of Hermas" was a proverb in Antioch; and soon men began to add to it, "Beautiful as the son of Hermas"; for the child developed swiftly in that favouring clime. At nine years of age he was straight and strong, firm of limb and clear of eye. His brown head was on a level with his father's heart. He was the jewel of the House of the Golden Pillars; the pride of Hermas, the new Fortunatus.

That year another drop of success fell into his brimming cup. His black Numidian horses, which he had been training for the world-renowned chariot-races of Antioch, won the victory over a score of rivals. Hermas received the prize carelessly from the judge's hands, and turned to drive once more around the circus, to show himself to the people. He lifted the eager boy into the chariot beside him to share his triumph.

Here, indeed, was the glory of his life—this matchless son, his brighter counterpart carved in breathing ivory, touching his arm, and balancing himself proudly on the swaying floor of the chariot. As the horses pranced around the ring, a great shout of applause filled the amphitheatre, and thousands of spectators waved their salutations of praise: "Hail, fortunate Hermas, master of success! Hail, little Hermas, prince of good luck!"

The sudden tempest of acclamation, the swift fluttering of innumerable garments in the air, startled the horses. They dashed violently forward, and plunged upon the bits. The left rein broke. They swerved to the right, swinging the chariot sideways with a grating noise, and dashing it against the stone parapet of the arena. In an instant the well was shattered. The axle struck the ground, and the chariot was dragged onward, rocking and staggering.

By a strenuous effort Hermas kept his place on the frail platform, clinging to the unbroken rein. But the boy was tossed lightly from his side at the first shock. His head struck the wall. And when Hermas turned to look for him, he was lying like a broken flower on the sand.

They carried the boy in a litter to the House of the Golden Pillars, summoning the most skillful physician of Antioch to attend him. For hours the child was as quiet as death. Hermas watched the white eyelids, folded close like lily-buds at night, even as one watches for the morning. At last they opened; but the fire of fever was burning in the eyes, and the lips were moving in a wild delirium.

Hour after hour that sweet childish voice rang through the halls and chambers of the splendid, helpless house, now rising in shrill calls of distress and senseless laughter, now sinking in weariness and dull moaning. The stars shone and faded; the sun rose and set; the roses bloomed and fell in the garden; the birds sang and slept among the jasmine-bowers. But in the heart of Hermas there was no song, no bloom, no light—only speechless anguish, and a certain fearful look-ing-for of desolation.

He was like a man in a nightmare. He saw the shapeless terror that was moving toward him, but he was impotent to stay or to escape it. He had done all that he could. There was nothing left but to wait.

He paced to and fro, now hurrying to the boy's bed as if he could not bear to be away from it, now turning back as if he could not endure to be near it. The people of the house, even Athenais, feared to speak to him, there was something so vacant and desperate in his face.

At nightfall on the second of those eternal days he shut himself in the library. The unfilled lamp had gone out, leaving a trail of smoke in the air. The sprigs of mignonette and rosemary, with which the room was sprinkled every day, were unrenewed, and scented the gloom with close odors of decay. A costly manuscript of Theocritus was tumbled in disorder on the floor. Hermas sank into a chair like a man in whom the very spring of being is broken. Through the darkness some one drew near. He did not even lift his head. A hand touched him; a soft arm was laid over his houlders. It was Athenais, kneeling beside him and speaking very low:

"Hermas—it is almost over—the child! His voice grows weaker hour by hour. He moans and calls for some one to help him; then he laughs. He breaks my heart. He has just fallen asleep. The moon is rising now. Unless a change comes he cannot last till sunrise. Is there nothing we can do? Is there no power that can save him? Is there no one to pity us and spare us? Let us call, let us beg for compassion and help; let us pray for his life!"

Yes; this was what he wanted—this was the only thing that could bring relief: to pray; to pour out his sorrow somewhere; to find a greater strength than his own and cling to it and plead for mercy and help. To leave this undone was to be false to his manhood; it was to be no better than the dumb beasts when their young perish. How could he let his boy suffer and die, without an effort, a cry, a prayer?

He sank on his knees beside Athenais.

"Out of the depths—out of the depths we call for pity. The light of our eyes is fading—the child is dying. Oh, the child, the child! Spare the child's life, thou merciful—"

Not a word; only that deathly blank. The hands of Hermas, stretched out in supplication, touched the marble table. He felt the cool hardness of the polished stone beneath his fingers. A roll of papyrus, dislodged by his touch, fell rustling to the floor. Through the open door, faint and far off, came the footsteps of the servants, moving cautiously. The heart of Hermas was like a lump of ice in his bosom. He rose slowly to his feet, lifting Athenais with him.

"It is in vain," he said. "There is nothing for us to do. Long ago I knew something. I think it would have helped us. But I have forgotten it. It is all gone. But I would give all that I have, if I could bring it back again now, at this hour, in this time of our bitter trouble."

A slave entered the room while he was speaking, and approached hesitatingly.

"Master," he said, "John of Antioch, whom we were forbidden to admit to the house, has come again. He would take no denial. Even now he waits in the hall; and the old man Marcion is with him, seeking to turn him away."

"Come," said Hermas to his wife, "let us go to him."

In the central hall the two men were standing; Marcion, with disdainful eyes and sneering lips, taunting the unbidden guest; John, silent, quiet, patient, while the wondering slaves looked on in dismay. He lifted his searching gaze to the haggard face of Hermas.

"My son, I knew that I should see you again, even though you did not send for me. I have come to you because I have heard that you are in trouble."

"It is true," answered Hermas, passionately. "We are in trouble, desperate trouble, trouble accursed. Our child is dying. We are poor, we are destitute, we are afflicted. In all this house, in all the world, there is no one that can help us. I knew something long ago, when I was with you—a word, a name—in which we might have found hope. But I have lost it. I gave it to this man. He has taken it away from me forever."

He pointed to Marcion. The old man's lips curled scornfully. "A word, a name!" he sneered. "What is that, O most wise man and holy

Presbyter? A thing of air, a thing that men make to describe their own dreams and fancies. Who would go about to rob anyone of such a thing as that? It is a prize that only a fool would think of taking. Besides, the young man parted with it of his own free will. He bargained with me cleverly. I promised him wealth and pleasure and fame. What did he give in return? An empty name, which was a burden—"

"Servant of demons, be still!" The voice of John rang clear, like a trumpet, through the hall. "There is a name which none shall dare to take in vain. There is a name which none can lose without being lost. There is a name at which the devils tremble. Go quickly, before I speak it!"

Marcion shrank into the shadow of one of the pillars. A lamp near him tottered on its pedestal and fell with a crash. In the confusion he vanished, as noiselessly as a shade.

John turned to Hermas, and his tone softened as he said, "My son, you have sinned deeper than you know. The word with which you parted so lightly is the key word of all life. Without it the world has no meaning, existence no peace, death no refuge. It is the word that purifies love, and comforts grief, and keeps hope alive forever. It is the most precious word that ever ear has heard, or mind has known, or heart has conceived. It is the name of Him who has given us life and breath and all things richly to enjoy; the name of Him who, though we may forget Him, never forgets us, the name of Him who pities us as you pity your suffering child; the name of Him who, though we wander far from Him, seeks us in the wilderness, and sent His Son, even as His Son has sent me this night, to breathe again that forgotten name in the heart that is perishing without it. Listen, my son, listen with all your soul to the blessed name of God our Father."

The cold agony in the breast of Hermas dissolved like a fragment of ice that melts in the summer sea. A sense of sweet release spread through him from head to foot. The lost was found. The dew of peace fell on his parched soul, and the withering flower of human love raised its head again. He stood upright, and lifted his hands high toward heaven.

"Out of the depths have I cried unto Thee, O Lord! O my God, be merciful to me, for my soul trusteth in Thee. My God, Thou hast given: take not Thy gift away from me, O my God! Spare the life of this my child, O Thou God, my Father, my Father!"

A deep hush followed the cry. "Listen!" whispered Athenais, breathlessly.

Was it an echo? It could not be, for it came again—the voice of the child, clear and low, waking from sleep, and calling: "Father!"

The Hero and the Tin Soldiers

n December twenty-fifth, 1918, that little white house in the park was certainly the happiest dwelling in Calvinton. It was simply running over with Christmas. You see, there had come to it a most wonderful present, a surprise full of tears and laughter. Captain Walter Mayne reached home on Christmas Eve.

For a while they had thought that he would never come back at all. News had been received that he was grievously wounded in France—shot to pieces, in effect, leading his men near Chateau-Thierry. His life hung on the ragged edge of those wounds. But his wife Katharine always believed that he would pull through. So he did. But he was lacking a leg, his right arm was knocked out of commission for the present, and various other souvenirs de la grande guerre were inscribed upon his body.

Then word arrived that he was coming on a transport, with other wounded, to be patched up in a hospital on Staten Island. So his wife Katharine smiled her way through innumerable entanglements of red tape and went to nurse him. Then she set her steady hand to pull all the wires necessary to get him discharged and sent home. Christmas was in her heart and she would not be denied. So it came to pass that the one-legged Hero was in his own house on the happy day, and joy was bubbling all around him.

When the old Pastor entered, late in the afternoon, the Christmas-tree was twinkling with lights, the children swarming and buzzing all over the place, so that he was dazed for a moment. There were Walter's mother and his aunt and his sisters-in-law, boys and girls of various sizes, and a jubilant and entrancing baby. The Pastor took it all in, and was glad of it, but his mind was on the Hero.

Katharine, who always understood everything, whispered softly, "Walter is waiting to see you, Doctor. He is in his study, just across the hall."

Waiting? Well, what can a man whose right leg has been cut off above the knee, and who has not yet been able to get an artificial one—what can he do but wait?

The room was rather dimly lighted; brilliance is not good for the eyes of the wounded. Walter was in a long chair in the corner; his face was bronzed, drawn and lined a little by suffering; but steady and cheerful as ever, with the eager look which had made his students listen to him when he talked to them about English literature.

"My dear Walter," said the Pastor, "my dear boy, we are so glad to have you home with us again. We are very proud of you. You are our Hero."

"Thank you," said Walter. "It is mighty good to be home again. But there is no hero business about it. I only did what all the other Americans who went over there did—fought my—excuse me, my best, against the beastly Germans."

"But your leg," said the Pastor impulsively, "it is gone. Aren't you angry about that?"

Walter was silent for a moment. Then he answered.

"No, I don't think angry is the right word. You remember that story about Nathan Hale in the Revolution—'I only regret that I have but one life to give to my country.' Well I'm glad that I had two legs to give for my country, and particularly glad that she only needed one of them."

"Tell me a bit about the fighting," said the Pastor, "I want to know what it was like—the hero-touch—you understand?"

"Not for me," said Walter, "and certainly not now. Later on I can tell you something, perhaps. But this is Christmas Day. And war? Well, Doctor, believe me, war is a horrible thing, full of grime and pain, madness, agony, hell—a thing that ought not to be. I have fought alongside of the other fellows to put an end to it, and now—"

The door swung open, and Sammy, the eldest son of the house, pranced in.

"Look, Daddy," he cried, "see what Aunt Emily has sent me for Christmas—a big box of tin soldiers!"

Mayne smiled as the little boy carefully laid the box on his knee; but there was a shadow of pain in his eyes, and he closed them for a few seconds, as if his mind were going back, somewhere, far away. Then he spoke, tenderly, but with a grave voice.

"That's fine, sonny—all those tin soldiers. But don't you think they ought to belong to me? You have lots of other toys, you know. Would you give the soldiers to me?"

The child looked up at him, puzzled for a moment; then a flash of comprehension passed over his face, and he nodded valiantly.

"Sure, Father," he said. "You're the Captain. Keep the soldiers. I'll play with the other toys," and he skipped out of the room.

Mayne's look followed him with love. Then he turned to the old Pastor and a strange expression came into his face, half whimsical and half grim.

"Doctor," he said, "will you do me a favor? Poke up that fire till it blazes. That's right. Now lay this box in the hottest part of the flames. That's right. It will soon be gone."

The elder man did what was asked, with an air of slight bewilderment, as one humours the fancies of an invalid. He wondered whether Mayne's fever had quite left him. He watched the fire bulging the lid and catching round the edges of the box. Then he heard Mayne's voice behind him, speaking very quietly.

"If ever I find my little boy playing with tin soldiers, I shall spank him well. No, that wouldn't be quite fair, would it? But I shall tell him why he must not do it, and I shall make him understand that it's an impossible thing."

Then the old Pastor comprehended. There was no touch of fever. The one-legged Hero had come home from the wars completely well and sound in mind. So the two men sat together in love by the Christmas fire, and saw the tin soldiers melt away.

A Christmas Prayer for the Home

Father of all men, look upon our family,
Kneeling together before Thee,
And grant us a true Christmas.

With loving heart we bless Thee:

    For the gift of Thy dear Son Jesus Christ,

    For the peace He brings to human homes,

    For the good-will He teaches to sinful men,

    For the glory of Thy goodness shining in His face.

With joyful voice we praise Thee:

    For His lowly birth and His rest in the manger,

    For the pure tenderness of His mother Mary,

    For the fatherly care that protected Him,

    For the providence that saved the Holy child

    To be the Saviour of the world.

With deep desire we beseech Thee:

    Help us to keep His birthday truly,

    Help us to offer, in His name, our Christmas prayer.

From the sickness of sin and the darkness of doubt,

From the selfish pleasures and sullen pains,

From the frost of pride and the fever of envy,

God save us every one, through the blessing of Jesus.

In the health of purity and the calm of mutual trust,
In the sharing of joy and the bearing of trouble,
In the steady glow of love and the clear light of hope,
God keep us every one, by the blessing of Jesus.

In praying and praising, in giving and receiving,
In eating and drinking, in singing and making merry,
In parents' gladness and in children's mirth,
In dear memories of those who have departed,
In good comradeship with those who are here,
In kind wishes for those who are far away,
In patient waiting, sweet contentment, generous cheer,
God bless us every one, with the blessing of Jesus.

By remembering our kindship with all men,
By well-wishing, friendly speaking and kindly doing,
By cheering the downcast and adding sunshine to daylight,
By welcoming strangers (poor shepherds or wise men),
By keeping the music of the angels' song in this home,
God help us every one to share the blessing of Jesus:

In whose name we keep Christmas,
And in whose words we pray together:

Our Father, which art in heaven, hallowed be Thy name,
Thy kingdom come. Thy will be done in earth, as it is in heaven.
Give us this day our daily bread. And forgive us our debts,
  as we forgive our debtors.
And lead us not into temptation, but deliver us from evil:
For Thine is the kingdom, and the power, and the glory, forever. Amen.

The Sad Shepherd

Darkness

ut of the Valley of Gardens, where a film of new-fallen snow lay smooth as feathers on the breast of a dove, the ancient Pools of Solomon looked up into the night sky with dark, tranquil eyes, wide-open and passive, reflecting the crisp stars and the small, round moon. The full springs, overflowing on the hill-side, melted their way through the field of white in winding channels, and along their course the grass was green even in the dead of winter.

But the sad shepherd walked far above the friendly valley, in a region where ridges of gray rock welted and scarred the back of the earth, like wounds of half-forgotten strife and battles long ago. The solitude was forbidding and disquieting; the keen air that searched the wanderer had no pity in it; and the myriad glances of the night were curiously cold.

His flock straggled after him. The sheep, weather beaten and dejected, followed the path with low heads nodding from side to side, as if they had travelled far and found little pasture. The black, lop-eared goats leaped upon the rocks, restless and ravenous, tearing down the tender branches and leaves of the dwarf oaks and wild olives.

They reared up against the twisted trunks and crawled and scrambled among the boughs. It was like a company of gray downcast friends and a troop of merry little black devils following the sad shepherd afar off.

He walked looking on the ground, paying small heed to them. Now and again, when the sound of pattering feet and panting breath and the rustling and rending among the copses fell too far behind, he drew out his shepherd's pipe and blew a strain of music, shrill and mournful, quavering and lamenting through the hollow night. He waited while the troops of gray and black scuffed and bounded and trotted near to him. Then he dropped the pipe into its place again and strode forward, looking on the ground.

The fitful, shivery wind that rasped the hill-top fluttered the rags of his long mantle of Tyrian blue, torn by thorns and stained by travel. The rich tunic of striped silk beneath it was worn thin, and the girdle about his loins had lost all its ornaments of silver and jewels. His curling hair hung down dishevelled under a turban of fine linen, in which the gilt threads were frayed and tarnished; and his shoes of soft leather were broken by the road. On his brown fingers the places of the vanished rings were still marked in white skin. He carried not the long staff nor the heavy nail-studded rod of the shepherd, but a slender stick of carved cedar battered and scratched by hard usage, and the handle, which must once have been of precious metal, was missing.

He was a strange figure for that lonely place and that humble occupation—a branch of faded beauty from some royal garden tossed by rude winds into the wilderness—a pleasure craft adrift, buffeted and broken, on rough seas.

But he seemed to have passed beyond caring. His young face was as frayed and threadbare as his garments. The splendour of the moonlight flooding the wide world meant as little to him as the hardness of the rugged track which he followed. He wrapped his tattered mantle closer to him, and strode ahead, looking on the ground.

As the path dropped from the summit of the ridge toward the Valley of Mills and passed among huge broken rocks, three men sprang at him from the shadows. He lifted his stick, but let it fall again, and a strange ghost of a smile twisted his face as they gripped him and threw him down.

"You are rough beggars," he said. "Say what you want, you are welcome to it."

"Your money, dog of a courtier," they muttered fiercely. "Give us your golden collar, Herod's hound, quick, or you die!"

"The quicker, the better," he answered, closing his eyes.

The bewildered flock of sheep and goats, gathered in a silent ring, stood at gaze while the robbers fumbled over their master.

"This is a stray dog," said one. "He has lost his collar, there is not even the price of a mouthful of wine on him. Shall we kill him and leave him for the vultures?"

"What have the vultures done for us," said another, "that we should feed them? Let us take his cloak and drive off his flock, and leave him to die in his own time."

With a kick and a curse they left him. He opened his eyes and lay quiet for a moment, with his twisted smile, watching the stars.

"You creep like snails," he said. "I thought you had marked my time to-night. But not even that is given to me for nothing. I must pay for all, it seems."

Far away, slowly scattering and receding, he heard the rustling and bleating of his frightened flock as the robbers, running and shouting, tried to drive them over the hills. Then he stood up and took the shepherd's pipe from the breast of his tunic. He blew again that sad, piercing air, sounding it out over the ridges and distant thickets. It seemed to have neither beginning nor end; a melancholy, pleading tune that searched forever after something lost.

While he played, the sheep and the goats, slipping away from their captors by roundabout ways, hiding behind the laurel bushes, following the dark gullies, leaping down the broken cliffs, came circling back to him, one after another; and as they came, he interrupted his playing, now and then, to call them by name.

When they were nearly all assembled, he went down swiftly toward the lower valley, and they followed him, panting. At the last crook of the path on the steep hillside a straggler came after him along the cliff. He looked up and saw it outlined against the sky. Then he saw it leap, and slip, and fall beyond the path into a deep cleft.

"Little fool," he said, "fortune is kind to you! You have escaped from the big trap of life. What? You are crying for help? You are still in the trap? Then I must go down to you, little fool, for I am a fool too. But why I must do it, I know no more than you know."

He lowered himself quickly and perilously into the cleft, and found the creature with its leg broken and bleeding. It was not a sheep, but a young goat. He had no cloak to wrap it in, but he took off his turban and unrolled it, and bound it around the trembling animal. Then he climbed back to the path and strode on at the head of his flock, carrying the little black kid in his arms.

There were houses in the Valley of the Mills; and in some of them lights were burning; and the drone of the mill-stones, where the women were still grinding, came out into the night like the humming of drowsy bees. As the women heard the pattering and bleating of the flock, they wondered who was passing so late. One of them, in a house where there was no mill but many lights, came to the door and looked out laughing, her face and bosom bare.

But the sad shepherd did not stay. His long shadow and the confused mass of lesser shadows behind him drifted down the white moonlight, past the yellow bars of lamplight that gleamed from the doorways. It seemed as if he were bound to go somewhere and would not delay.

Yet with all his haste to be gone, it was plain that he thought little of where he was going. For when he came to the foot of the valley, where the paths divided, he stood between them staring vacantly, without a desire to turn him this way or that. The imperative of choice halted him like a barrier. The balance of his mind hung even because both scales were empty. He could act, he could go, for his strength was untouched; but he could not choose, for his will was broken within him.

The path to the left went up toward the little town of Bethlehem, with huddled roofs and walls in silhouette along the double-crested hill. It was dark and forbidding as a closed fortress. The sad shepherd looked at it with indifferent eyes; there was nothing there to draw him.

The path to the right wound through rock-strewn valleys toward the Dead Sea. But rising out of that crumpled wilderness, a mile or two away, the smooth white ribbon of a chariot-road lay upon the flank of a cone-shaped mountain and curled in loops toward its peak. There the great cone was cut squarely off, and the levelled summit was capped by a palace of marble, with round towers at the corners and flaring beacons along the walls; and the glow of an immense fire, hidden in the central courtyard, painted a false dawn in the eastern sky. All down the clean-cut mountain slopes, on terraces and blind arcades, the lights flashed from lesser pavilions and pleasure-houses.

It was the secret orchard of Herod and his friends, their trysting-place with the spirits of mirth and madness. They called it the Mountain of the Little Paradise. Rich gardens were there; and the cool water from the Pools of Solomon splashed in the fountains; and trees of the knowledge of good and evil fruited blood-red and ivory-white above them; and smooth, curving, glistening shapes, whispering softly of pleasures, lay among the flowers and glided behind the trees. All this was now hidden in the dark. Only the strange bulk of the mountain, a sharp black pyramid girdled and crowded with fire, loomed across the night—a mountain once seen never to be forgotten.

The sad shepherd remembered it well. He looked at it with the eyes of a child who had been in hell. It burned him from afar. Turning neither to the right nor to the left, he walked without a path straight out upon the plain of Bethlehem, still whitened in the hollows and on the sheltered side of its rounded hillocks by the veil of snow.

He faced a wide and empty world. To the west in sleeping Bethlehem, to the east in flaring Herodium, the life of man was infinitely far away from him. Even the stars seemed to withdraw themselves against the blue-black of the sky. They diminished and receded till they were like pinholes in the vault above him. The moon in mid-heaven shrank into a bit of burnished silver, hard and glittering, immeasurably remote. The ragged, inhospitable ridges of Tekoa lay stretched in mortal slumber along the horizon, and between them he caught a glimpse of the sunken Lake of Death, darkly gleaming in its deep bed. There was no movement, no sound, on the plain where he walked, except the soft-padding feet of his dumb, obedient flock.

He felt an endless isolation strike cold to his heart, against which he held the limp body of the wounded kid, wondering the while, with a half-contempt for his own foolishness, why he took such trouble to save a tiny scrap of the worthless tissue which is called life.

Even when a man does not know or care where he is going, if he steps onward he will get there. In an hour or more of walking over the plain, the sad shepherd came to a sheep-fold of grey stones with a rude tower beside it. The fold was full of sheep, and at the foot of the tower a little fire of thorns was burning, around which four shepherds were crouching, wrapped in their thick woolen cloaks.

As the stranger approached them they looked up, and one of them rose quickly to his feet, grasping his knotted club. But when they saw the flock that followed the sad shepherd, they stared at each other and said: "It is one of us, a keeper of sheep. But how comes he here in this raiment? It is what men wear in kings' houses."

"No," said the one who was standing. "It is what they wear when they have been thrown out of them. Look at the rags. He may be a thief and robber with his stolen flock."

"Salute him when he comes near," said the oldest shepherd. "Are we not four to one? We have nothing to fear from a ragged traveller. Speak him fair. It is the will of God—and it costs nothing."

"Peace be with you, brother," cried the youngest shepherd. "May your mother and father be blessed."

"May your heart be enlarged," the stranger answered, "and may all your families be more blessed than mine, for I have none."

"A homeless man," said the old shepherd, "has either been robbed by his fellows, or punished by God."

"I do not know which it was," answered the stranger. "The end is the same, as you see."

"By your speech you come from Galilee. Where are you going? What are you seeking here?"

"I was going nowhere, my masters; but it was cold on the way there, and my feet turned to your fire."

"Come then, if you are a peaceable man, and warm your feet with us. Heat is a good gift; divide it and it is not less. But you shall have bread and salt too, if you will."

"May your hospitality enrich you. I am your unworthy servant. But my flock?"

"Let your flock shelter by the south wall of the fold; there is good picking there and no wind. Come you and sit with us."

So they all sat down by the fire; and the sad shepherd ate of their bread, but sparingly, like a man to whom hunger brings a need but no joy in the satisfying of it; and the others were silent for a proper time, out of courtesy. Then the oldest shepherd spoke:

"My name is Zadok the son of Eliezer, of Bethlehem. I am the chief shepherd of the flocks of the Temple, which are before you in the fold. These are my sister's sons, Jotham and Shama, and Nathan: their father Elkanah is dead; and but for these I am a childless man."

"My name," replied the stranger, "is Ammiel the son of Jochanan, of the city of Bethsaida, by the Sea of Galilee, and I am a fatherless man."

"It is better to be childless than fatherless," said Zadok, "yet it is the will of God that children should bury their fathers. When did the blessed Jochanan die?"

"I know not whether he be dead or alive. It is three years since I looked upon his face or had word of him."

"You are an exile, then? He has cast you off?"

"It was the other way," said Ammiel, looking on the ground.

At this the shepherd Shama, who had listened with doubt in his face, started up in anger. "Pig of a Galilean," he cried, "despiser of parents! Breaker of the law! When I saw you coming I knew you for something vile. Why do you darken the night for us with your presence? You have reviled him who begot you. Away, or we stone you!"

Ammiel did not answer or move. The twisted smile passed over his face again as he waited to know the shepherd's will with him, even as he had waited for the robbers. But Zadok lifted his hand.

"Not so hasty, Shama-ben-Elkanah. You also break the law by judging a man unheard. The rabbis have told us that there is a tradition

124

of the elders—a rule as holy as the law itself—that a man may deny his father in a certain way without sin. It is a strange rule, and it must be very holy or it would not be so strange. But this is the teaching of the elders: a son may say of anything for which his father asks him— a sheep, or a measure of corn, or a field, or a purse of silver—'it is Corban, a gift that I have vowed unto the Lord'; and so his father shall have no more claim upon him. Have you said 'Corban' to your father, Ammiel-ben-Jochanan? Have you made a vow unto the Lord?"

"I have said 'Corban,'" answered Ammiel, lifting his face, still shadowed by that strange smile, "but it was not the Lord who heard my vow."

"Tell us what you have done," said the old man sternly, "for we will neither judge you, nor shelter you, unless we hear your story."

"There is nothing in it," replied Ammiel indifferently. "It is an old story. But if you are curious you shall hear it. Afterward you shall deal with me as you will."

So the shepherds, wrapped in their warm cloaks, sat listening with grave faces and watchful, unsearchable eyes, while Ammiel in his tattered silk sat by the sinking fire of thorns and told his tale with a voice that had no room for hope or fear—a cool, dead voice that spoke only of things ended.

Nightfire

"In my father's house I was the second son. My brother was honored and trusted in all things. He was a prudent man and profitable to the household. All that he counselled was done, all that he wished he had. My place was a narrow one. There was neither honor nor joy in it, for it was filled with daily tasks and rebukes. No one cared for me. My mother sometimes wept when I was rebuked. Perhaps she was disappointed in me. But she had no power to make things better. I felt that I was a beast of burden, fed only in order that I might be useful; and the dull life irked me like an ill-fitting harness. There was nothing in it.

"I went to my father and claimed my share of the inheritance. He was rich. He gave it to me. It did not improvish him and it made me free. I said to him 'Corban' and shook the dust of Bethsaida from my feet.

"I went out to look for mirth and love and joy and all that is pleasant to the eyes and sweet to the taste. If a god made me, thought I, he made me to live, and the pride of life was strong in my heart and in my flesh. My vow was offered to that well-known god. I served him in Jerusalem, in Alexandria, in Rome, for his altars are everywhere and men worship him openly or in secret.

"My money and youth made me welcome to his followers, and I spent them both freely as if they could never come to an end. I clothed myself in purple and fine linen and fared sumptuously every day. The wine of Cyprus and the dishes of Egypt and Syria were on my table. My dwelling was crowded with merry guests. They came for what I gave them. Their faces were hungry and their soft touch was like the clinging of leeches. To them I was nothing but money and youth; no longer a beast of burden—a beast of pleasure. There was nothing in it.

"From the richest fare my heart went away empty, and after the wildest banquet my soul fell drunk and solitary into sleep.

"Then I thought, power is better than pleasure. If a man will feast and revel let him do it with the great. They will favour him and raise him up for the services he renders them. He will obtain place and authority in the world and gain many friends. So I joined myself with Herod."

When the sad shepherd spoke this name his listeners drew back from him as if it were a defilement to hear it. They spat upon the ground and cursed the Idumean who called himself their king.

"A slave!" Jotham cried, "A bloody tyrant and a slave from Edom! A fox, a vile beast who devours his own children! God burn him in Gehenna!"

The old Zadok picked up a stone and threw it into the darkness, saying slowly, "I cast this stone on the grave of the Idumean, the blasphemer, the defiler of the Temple! God send us soon the Deliverer, the Promised One, the true King of Israel!" Ammiel made no sign, but went on with his story.

"Herod used me well—for his own purpose. He welcomed me to his palace and his table, and gave me a place among his favorites. He was so much my friend that he borrowed my money. There were many of the nobles of Jerusalem with him, Saducees, and proselytes from Rome and Asia, and women from everywhere. The law of Israel was observed in the open court, when the people were watching. But in the secret feasts there was no law but the will of Herod, and many deities were served but no god was worshipped. There the captains and the princes of Rome consorted with the high-priest and his sons by night; and there was much coming and going by hidden ways. Everybody was a borrower or a seller of favors. It was a house of diligent madness. There was nothing in it.

"In the midst of this whirling life a great need of love came upon me and I wished to love someone in my inmost heart.

"At a certain place in the city, within closed doors, I saw a young slave-girl dancing. She was about fifteen years old, thin and supple; she danced like a reed in the wind; but her eyes were weary as death, and her white body was marked with bruises. She stumbled and the men laughed at her. She fell and her mistress beat her, crying out that she would fain be rid of such a heavy-footed slave. I paid the price and took her to my dwelling.

"Her name was Tamar. She was a daughter of Lebanon. I robed her in silk and broidered linen. I nourished her with tender care so that beauty came upon her like the blossoming of an almond tree; she was a garden enclosed, breathing spices. Her eyes were like doves behind her veil, her lips were a thread of scarlet, her neck was a tower of ivory, and her breasts were as two fawns which feed among the lilies. She was whiter than milk, and more rosy than the flower of the peach, and her dancing was like the flight of a bird among the branches. So I loved her.

"She lay in my bosom as a clear stone that one has bought and polished and set in fine gold at the end of a golden chain. Never was she glad at my coming, or sorry at my going. Never did she give me anything except what I took from her. There was nothing in it.

"Now whether Herod knew of the jewel I kept in my dwelling I cannot tell. It was sure that he had his spies in all the city, and himself walked the streets by night in a disguise. On a certain day he sent for me, and had me into his secret chamber, professing great love toward me and more confidence than in any man that lived. So I must go to Rome for him, bearing a sealed letter and a private message for Caesar. All my goods would be left safely in the hands of the king, my friend, who would reward me double. There was a certain place of high authority at Jerusalem which Caesar would gladly bestow on a Jew who had done him a service. This mission would commend me to him. It was a great occasion, suited to my powers. Thus Herod fed me with fair promises, and I ran his errand. There was nothing in it.

"I stood before Caesar and gave him the letter. He read it and laughed, saying that a prince with an incurable hunger is a servant of value to an emperor. Then he asked me if there was nothing sent with the letter. I answered that there was no gift, but a message for his private ear. He drew me aside and I told him that Herod begged earnestly that his dear son, Antipater, might be sent back in haste from Rome to Palestine, for the king had great need of him.

"At this, Caesar laughed again. 'To bury him, I suppose,' he said, 'with his brothers, Alexander and Aristobulus! Truly, it is better to be Herod's swine than his son! Tell the old fox that he may catch his own prey.' With that he turned from me and I withdrew unrewarded, to make my way back, as best I could with an empty purse, to Palestine. I had seen the Lord of the World. There was nothing in it.

"Selling my rings and bracelets I got passage in a trading ship for Joppa. There I heard that the king was not in Jerusalem, at his Palace of the Upper City, but had gone with his friends to make merry for a month on the Mountain of Little Paradise. On that hill-top over against us, where the lights are flaring to-night, in the banquet-hall where couches are spread for a hundred guests, I found Herod."

The listening shepherds spat upon the ground again, and Jotham muttered, "May the worms that devour his flesh never die!" But Zadok whispered, "We wait for the Lord's salvation to come out of Zion." And the sad shepherd, looking with fixed eyes at the firelit mountain far away, continued his story:

"The king lay on his ivory couch, and the sweat of his disease was heavy upon him, for he was old, and his flesh was corrupted. But his hair and his beard were dyed and perfumed and there was a wreath of roses on his head. The hall was full of nobles and great men, the sons of the high-priest were there, and the servants poured their wine in cups of gold. There was a sound of soft music; and all the men were watching a girl who danced in the middle of the hall; and the eyes of Herod were fiery, like the eyes of a fox.

"The dancer was Tamar. She glistened like the snow on Lebanon, and the redness of her was ruddier than a pomegranate, and her dancing was like the coiling of white serpents. When the dance was ended her attendants threw a veil of gauze over her and she lay among her cushions, half covered with flowers, at the feet of the king.

"Through the sound of clapping hands and shouting, two slaves led me behind the couch of Herod. His eyes narrowed as they fell upon me. I told him the message of Caesar, making it soft, as if it were a word that suffered him to catch his prey. He stroked his beard and his look fell on Tamar. 'I have caught it,' he murmured; 'by all the gods, I have always caught it. And my dear son, Antipater, is coming home of his own free will. I have lured him, he is mine.'

"Then a look of madness crossed his face and he sprang up, with frothing lips, and struck at me. 'What is this,' he cried, 'a spy, a servant of my false son, a traitor in my banquet-hall! Who are you?' I knelt before him, protesting that he must know me; that I was his friend, his messenger; that I had left all my goods in his hands; that the girl who had danced for him was mine. At this his face changed again and he fell back on his couch, shaken with horrible laughter. 'Yours!' he cried. 'When was she yours? What is yours? I know you now, poor madman. You are Ammiel, a crazy shepherd from Galilee, who troubled us some time since. Take him away, slaves. He has twenty sheep and twenty goats among my flock at the foot of the mountain. See to it that he gets them, and drive him away.'

"I fought against the slaves with my bare hands, but they held me. I called to Tamar, begging her to have pity on me, to speak for me, to come with me. She looked up with her eyes like doves behind her veil, but there was no knowledge of me in them. She laughed lazily, as if it were a poor comedy, and flung a broken rose-branch in my face. Then the silver cord was loosened within me, and my heart went out, and I struggled no more. There was nothing in it.

"Afterward I found myself on the road with this flock. I led them past Hebron into the south country, and so by the Vale of Eshcol, and over many hills beyond the Pools of Solomon, until my feet brought me to your fire. Here I rest on the way to nowhere."

He sat silent, and the four shepherds looked at him with amazement.

"It is a bitter tale," said Shama, "and you are a great sinner."

"I should be a fool not to know that," answered the sad shepherd, "but the knowledge does me no good."

"You must repent," said Nathan, the youngest shepherd, in a friendly voice.

"How can a man repent," answered the sad shepherd, "unless he has hope? But I am sorry for everything, and most of all for living."

"Would you not live to kill the fox Herod?" cried Jotham fiercely.

"Why should I let him out of the trap?" answered the sad shepherd. "Is he not dying more slowly than I could kill him?"

"You must have faith in God," said Zadok earnestly and gravely.

"He is too far away."

"Then you must have love for your neighbour."

"He is too near. My confidence in man was like a pool by the wayside. It was shallow, but there was water in it, and sometimes a star shone there. Now the feet of many beasts have trampled through it, and the jackals have drunken of it, and there is no more water. It is dry and the mire is caked at the bottom."

"Is there nothing good in the world?"

"There is pleasure, but I am sick of it. There is power, but I hate it. There is wisdom, but I mistrust it. Life is a game and every player is for his own hand. Mine is played. I have nothing to win or lose."

"You are young; you have many years to live."

"I am old, yet the days before me are too many."

"But you travel the road, you go forward. Do you hope for nothing?"

"I hope for nothing," said the sad shepherd. "Yet if one thing should come to me, it might be the beginning of hope. If I saw in man or woman a deed of kindness without a selfish reason, and a proof of love gladly given for its own sake only, then might I turn my face toward that light. Till that comes, how can I have faith in God whom I have never seen? I have seen the world which he has made, and it brings me no faith. There is nothing in it."

"Ammiel-ben-Jochanan," said the old man sternly, "you are a son of Israel, and we have had compassion on you, according to the law. But you are an apostate, an unbeliever, and we can have no more fellowship with you, lest a curse come upon us. The company of the desperate brings misfortune. Go your way and depart from us, for our way is not yours."

So the sad shepherd thanked them for their entertainment, and took the little kid again in his arms, and went into the night, calling his flock. But the youngest shepherd Nathan followed him a few steps and said, "There is a broken fold at the foot of the hill. It is old and small, but you may find a shelter there for your flock where the wind will not shake you. Go your way with God, brother, and see better days."

Then Ammiel went a little way down the hill and sheltered his flock in a corner of the crumbling walls. He lay among the sheep and the goats with his face upon his folded arms, and whether the time passed slowly or swiftly he did not know, for he slept.

He waked as Nathan came running and stumbling among the scattered stone.

"We have seen a vision," he cried, "a wonderful vision of angels. Did you not hear them? They sang loudly of the Hope of Israel. We are going to Bethlehem to see this thing which is come to pass. Come you and keep watch over our sheep while we are gone."

"Of angels I have seen and heard nothing," said Ammiel, "but I will guard your flocks with mine, since I am in debt to you for your bread and fire."

So he brought the kid in his arms, and the weary flock straggling after him, to the south wall of the great fold again, and sat there by embers at the foot of the tower, while the others were away.

The moon rested like a ball on the edge of the western hills and rolled behind them. The stars faded in the east and the fires went out on the Mountain of the Little Paradise. Over the hills of Moab, a gray flood of dawn rose slowly, and arrows of red shot far up before the sunrise.

The shepherds returned full of joy and told what they had seen.

"It was even as the angels said unto us," said Shama, "and it must be true. The King of Israel has come. The faithful shall be blessed."

"Herod shall fall," cried Jotham, lifting his clenched fist toward the dark mountain. "Burn, black Idumean, in the bottomless pit, where the fire is not quenched."

Zadok spoke more quietly. "We found the new-born child of whom the angels told us wrapped in swaddling clothes and lying in a manger. The ways of God are wonderful. His salvation comes out of darkness. But you, Ammiel-ben-Jochanan, except you believe, you shall not see it. Yet since you have kept our flocks faithfully, and because of the joy that has come to us, I give you this piece of silver to help you on your way."

But Nathan came close to the sad shepherd and touched him on the shoulder with a friendly hand. "Go you also to Bethlehem," he said in a low voice, "for it is good to see what we have seen, and we will keep your flock until you return."

"I will go," said Ammiel, looking into his face, "for I think you wish me well. But whether I shall see what you have seen, or whether I shall ever return, I know not. Farewell."

Dawn

The narrow streets of Bethlehem were waking to the first stir of life as the sad shepherd came into the town with the morning, and passed through them like one walking in his sleep.

The courtyard of the great inn and the open rooms around it were crowded with travellers, rousing from their night's rest and making ready for the day's journey. In front of the stables half hollowed in the rock beside the inn, men were saddling their horses and their beasts of burden, and there was much noise and confusion.

But beyond these, at the end of the line, there was a deeper grotto in the rock, which was used only when the nearer stalls were full. Beside the entrance of this cave, an ass was tethered, and a man of middle age stood in the doorway.

The sad shepherd saluted him and told his name.

"I am Joseph the carpenter of Nazareth," replied the man. "Have you also seen the angels of whom your brother shepherds came to tell us?"

"I have seen no angels," answered Ammiel, "nor have I any brothers among the shepherds. But I would fain see what they have seen."

"It is our first-born son," said Joseph, "and the Most High has sent him to us. He is a marvellous child; great things are foretold of him. You may go in, but quietly, for the child and his mother Mary are asleep."

So the sad shepherd went in quietly. His long shadow entered before him, for the sunrise was flowing into the door of the grotto. It was clean and put in order, and a bed of straw was laid in the corner on the ground.

The child was asleep, but the young mother was waking, for she had taken him from the manger into her lap, where her maiden veil of white was spread to receive him. And she was singing very softly as she bent over him in wonder and content.

Ammiel saluted her and kneeled down to look at the child. He saw nothing different from other young children. The mother waited for him to speak of angels, as the other shepherds had done. The sad shepherd did not speak, but only looked. And as he looked, his face changed.

"You have suffered pain and danger and sorrow for his sake," he said gently.

"They are past," she answered, "and for his sake I have suffered them gladly."

"He is very little and helpless; you must bear many troubles for his sake."

"To care for him is my joy, and to bear him lightens my burden."

"He does not know you; he can do nothing for you."

"But I know him. I have carried him under my heart. He is my son and my king."

"Why do you love him?"

The mother looked up at the sad shepherd with a great reproach in her soft eyes. Then her look grew pitiful as it rested on his face.

"You are a sorrowful man," she said.

"I am a wicked man," he answered.

She shook her head gently.

"I know nothing of that," she said, "but you must be very sorrowful, since you are born of a woman and yet you ask a mother

135

why she loves her child. I love him for love's sake, because God has given him to me."

So the mother Mary leaned over her little son again and began to croon a song as if she were alone with him.

But Ammiel was still there, watching and thinking and beginning to remember. It came back to him that there was a woman in Galilee who had wept when he was rebuked; whose eyes had followed him when he was unhappy, as if she longed to do something for him; whose voice had broken and dropped silent while she covered her tear-stained face when he went away.

His thoughts flowed swiftly and silently toward her and after her like rapid waves of light. There was a thought of her bending over a little child in her lap, singing softly for pure joy—and the child was himself. There was a thought of her lifting a little child to the breast that had borne him as a burden and a pain, to nourish him there as a comfort and a treasure—and the child was himself. There was a thought of her watching and tending and guiding a little child from day to day, from year to year, putting tender arms around him, bending over his first wavering steps, rejoicing in his joys, wiping away the tears from his eyes, as he had never tried to wipe her tears away—and the child was himself. She had done everything for the child's sake, but what had the child done for her sake? And the child was himself; that was what he had come to—after the nightfire had burned out, after the darkness had grown thin and melted in the thoughts that pulsed through it like rapid waves of light—that was what he had come to in the early morning—himself, a child in his mother's arms.

Then he arose and went out of the grotto softly, making the three-fold sign of reverence; and the eyes of Mary followed him with kind looks.

Joseph of Nazareth was still waiting outside the door.

"How was it that you did not see the angels?" he asked. "Were you not with the other shepherds?"

"No," answered Ammiel, "I was asleep. But I have seen the mother and the child. Blessed be the house that holds them."

"You are strangely clad for a shepherd," said Joseph. "Where do you come from?"

"From a far country," said Ammiel. "From a country that you have never visited."

"Where are you going now?" asked Joseph.

"I am going home," answered Ammiel, "to my mother's and my father's house in Galilee."

"Go in peace, friend," said Joseph.

And the sad shepherd took up his battered staff, and went on his way rejoicing.

The Christmas Angel

t was the hour of rest in the Country Beyond the Stars. All the silver bells that swing with the turning of the great ring of light which lies around that land were softly chiming; and the sound of their commotion went down like dew upon the golden ways of the city, and the long alleys of blossoming trees, and the meadows of asphodel, and the curving shores of the River of Life.

At the hearing of that chime, all the angels who had been working turned to play, and all who had been playing gave themselves joyfully to work. Those who had been singing, and making melody on different instruments, fell silent and began to listen. Those who had been walking alone in meditation met together in companies to talk. And those who had been far away on errands to the Earth and other planets came homeward like a flight of swallows to the high cliff when the day is over.

It was not that they needed to be restored from weariness, for the inhabitants of that country never say, "I am tired." But there, as here, the law of change is the secret of happiness, and the joy that never ends is woven of mingled strands of labor and repose, society and solitude, music and silence. Sleep comes to them not as it does to us, with a darkening of the vision and a folding of the wings of the spirit, but with an opening of the eyes to deeper and fuller light, and with an effortless outgoing of the soul upon broader currents of life, as the sun-loving bird poises and circles upward, without a wing-beat, on the upholding air.

It was in one of the quiet corners of the green valley called Peacefield, where the little brook of Brighthopes runs smoothly down to join the River of Life, that I saw a company of angels, returned from various labors on Earth, sitting in friendly converse on the hill-side, where cyclamens and arbutus and violets and fringed orchids and pale lady's-tresses, and all the sweet-smelling flowers which are separated in the lower world by the seasons, were thrown together in a harmony of fragrance. There were three of the company who seemed to be leaders, distinguished not only by more radiant and powerful looks, but by a tone of authority in their speech and by the willing attention with which the others listened to them, as they talked of their earthly tasks, of the tangles and troubles, the wars and miseries that they had seen among men, and of the best way to get rid of them and bring sorrow to an end.

"The Earth is full of oppression and unrighteousness," said the tallest and most powerful of the angels. His voice was deep and strong, and by his shining armor and the long two-handed sword hanging over his shoulder I knew that he was the archangel Michael, the mightiest one among the warriors of the King, and the executor of the divine judgments upon the unjust. "The Earth is tormented with injustice," he cried, "and the great misery that I have seen among men is that the evil hand is often stronger than the good hand and can beat it down.

"The arm of the cruel is heavier than the arm of the kind. The unjust get the better of the just and tread on them. I have seen tyrant kings crush their helpless folk. I have seen the fields of the innocent trampled into bloody ruin by the feet of conquering armies. I have seen the wicked nation overcome the peoples that loved liberty, and take away their treasure by force of arms. I have seen poverty mocked by arrogant wealth, and purity deflowered by brute violence, and gentleness and fair-dealing bruised in the winepress of iniquity and pride.

"There is no cure for this evil, but by the giving of greater force to the good hand. The righteous cause must be strengthened with might to resist the wicked, to defend the helpless, to punish all cruelty and unfairness, to uphold the right everywhere, and to enforce justice with unconquerable arms. Oh, that the host of Heaven might be called, arrayed, and sent to mingle in the wars of men, to make the good victorious, to destroy all evil, and to make the will of the King prevail!

"We would shake down the thrones of tyrants, and loose the bands of the oppressed. We would hold the cruel and violent with the bit of fear, and drive the greedy and fierce-minded men with the whip of terror. We would stand guard, with weapons drawn, about the innocent, the gentle, the kind, and keep the peace of God with the sword of the angels!"

As he spoke, his hands were lifted to the hilt of his long blade, and he raised it above him, straight and shining, throwing the sparkles of light around it, like the spray from the sharp prow of a moving ship. Bright flames of heavenly ardor leaped in the eyes of the listening angels: a martial air passed over their faces as if they longed for the call to war. But no silver trumpet blared from the battlements of the City of God; no crimson flag was unfurled on those high, secret walls; no thrilling drum-beat echoed over the smooth meadow. Only the sound of the brook of Brighthopes was heard tinkling and murmuring among the roots of the grasses and flowers; and far off a cadence of song drifted down from the inner courts of the Palace of the King.

Then another angel began to speak, and made answer to Michael. He, too, was tall and wore the look of power. But it was power of the mind rather than of the hand. His face was clear and glistening, and his eyes were lit with a steady flame which neither leaped nor fell. Of flame also were his garments, which clung about him as the fire enwraps a torch burning where there is no wind; and his great wings, spiring to a point far above his head, were like a living lamp before the altar of the Most High. By this sign I knew that it was the archangel Uriel, the spirit of the Sun, clearest in vision, deepest in wisdom of all the spirits that surround the throne. "I hold not the same thought," said he, "as the great archangel Michael; nor, though I desire the same end which he desires, would I seek it by the same way. For I know how often power has been given to the good, and how often it has been turned aside and used for evil. I know that the host of Heaven, and the very stars in their courses, have fought on the side of a favoured nation; yet pride has followed triumph and oppression has been the first-born child of victory. I know that the deliverers of the people have become tyrants over those whom they have set free, and the fighters for liberty have been changed into the soldiers of fortune. Power corrupts itself, and might cannot save.

"Does not the Prince Michael remember how the angel of the Lord led the armies of Israel, and gave them the battle against every foe, except the enemy within the camp? And how they robbed and crushed the peoples against whom they had fought for freedom? And how the wickedness of the tribes of Canaan survived their conquest and overcame their conquerors, so that the children of Israel learned to worship the idols of their enemies, Moloch, and Baal, and Ashtoreth?

"Power corrupts itself, and might cannot save. Was not Persia the destroyer of Babylon, and did not the tyranny of Persia cry aloud for destruction? Did not Rome break the yoke of the East, and does not the yoke of Rome lie heavy on the shoulders of the world? Listen!"

There was silence for a moment on the slopes of Peacefield, and then over the encircling hills a cool wind brought the sound of chains clanking in prisons and galleys, the sighing of millions of slaves, the weeping of wretched women and children, the blows of hammers nailing men to their crosses. Then the sound passed by with the wind, and Uriel spoke again:

"Power corrupts itself, and might cannot save. The Earth is full of ignorant strife, and for this evil there is no cure but by the giving of greater knowledge. It is because men do not understand evil that they yield themselves to its power. Wickedness is folly in action, and injustice is the error of the blind. It is because men are ignorant that they destroy one another, and at last themselves.

"If there were more light in the world there would be no sorrow. If the great King who knows all things would enlighten the world with wisdom—wisdom to understand his law and his ways, to read the secrets of the earth and the stars, to discern the workings of the heart of man and the things that make for joy and peace—if he would but send us, his messengers, as a flame of fire to shine upon those who sit in darkness, how gladly would we go to bring in the new day!

"We would speak the word of warning and counsel to the erring, and tell knowledge to the perplexed. We would guide the ignorant in the paths of prudence, and the young would sit at our feet and hear us gladly in the school of life. Then folly would fade away as the morning vapor, and the sun of wisdom would shine on all men, and the peace of God would come with the counsel of the angels."

A murmur of pleasure followed the words of Uriel, and eager looks flashed around the circle of the messengers of light as they heard the praise of wisdom fitly spoken. But there was one among them on

143

whose face a shadow of doubt rested, and though he smiled, it was as if he remembered something that the others had forgotten. He turned to an angel near him.

"Who was it," said he, "to whom you were sent with counsel long ago? Was it not Balaam the son of Beor, as he was riding to meet the King of Moab? And did not even the dumb beast profit more by your instruction than the man who rode him? And who was it," he continued, turning to Uriel, "that was called the wisest of all men, having searched out and understood the many inventions that are found under the sun? Was not Solomon, prince of fools and philosophers, unable by much learning to escape weariness of the flesh and despair of the spirit? Knowledge also is vanity and vexation. This I know well, because I have dwelt among men and held converse with them since the day when I was sent to instruct the first man in Eden."

Then I looked more closely at him who was speaking and recognized the beauty of the archangel Raphael, as it was pictured long ago:

> A seraph winged; six wings he wore to shade
> His lineaments divine; the pair that clad
> Each shoulder broad came mantling o'er his breast,
> With regal ornament; the middle pair
> Girt like a starry zone his waist, and round
> Skirted his loins and thighs with downy gold
> And colors dipped in Heav'n; the third his feet
> Shadowed from either heel with feathered mail,
> Sky-tinctured grain. Like Maia's son he stood
> And shook his plumes, that Heavenly fragrance filled
> The circuit wide.

"Too well I know," he spoke on, while the smile on his face deepened into a look of pity and tenderness and desire. "Too well I know that power corrupts itself and that knowledge cannot save. There is no cure for the evil that is in the world but by the giving of more love to men. The laws that are ordained for earth are strange and unequal, and the ways where men must walk are full of pitfalls and dangers. Pestilence creeps along the ground and flows in the rivers; whirlwind and tempest shake the habitations of men and drive their ships to destruction; fire breaks forth from the mountains and the foundations of the world tremble. Frail is the flesh of man, and many are his pains and troubles. His children can never find peace until they learn to love one another and to help one another.

"Wickedness is begotten by disease and misery. Violence comes from poverty and hunger. The cruelty of oppression is when the strong tread the weak under their feet; the bitterness of pride is when the wise and learned despise the simple; the crown of folly is when the rich think they are gods, and the poor think that God is not.

"Hatred and envy and contempt are the curse of life. And for these there is no remedy save love—the will to give and to bless—the will of the King himself, who gives to all and is loving unto every man. But how shall the hearts of men be won to this will? How shall it enter into them and possess them? Even the gods that men fashion for themselves are cruel and proud and false and unjust. How shall the miracle be wrought in human nature to reveal the meaning of humanity? How shall men be made like God?"

At this question a deep hush fell around the circle, and every listener was still, even as the rustling leaves hang motionless when the light breeze falls away in the hour of sunset. Then through the silence, like the song of a far-away thrush from its hermitage in the forest, a voice came ringing: "I know it, I know it, I know it."

Clear and sweet—clear as a ray of light, sweeter than the smallest silver bell that rang the hour of rest—was that slender voice floating on the odorous and translucent air. Nearer and nearer it came, echoing down the valley, "I know it, I know it, I know it!"

Then from between the rounded hills, among which the brook of Brighthopes is born, appeared a young angel, a little child, with flying hair of gold, and green wreaths twined about his shoulders, and fluttering hands that played upon the air and seemed to lift him so lightly that he had no need of wings. As thistle-down, blown by the wind, dances across the water, so he came along the little stream, singing clear above the murmur of the brook.

All the angels rose and turned to look at him with wondering eyes. Multitudes of others came flying swiftly to the place from which the strange, new song was sounding. Rank within rank, like a garden of living flowers, they stood along the sloping banks of the brook while the child-angel floated into the midst of them, singing:

"I know it, I know it, I know it! Man shall be made like God because the Son of God shall become a man."

At this all the angels looked at one another with amazement, and gathered more closely about the child-angel, as those who hear wonderful news.

"How can this be?" they asked. "How is it posible that the Son of God should be a man?"

"I do not know," said the young angel. "I only know that it is to be."

"But if he becomes a man," said Raphael, "he will be at the mercy of men; the cruel and the wicked will have power upon him; he will suffer."

"I know it," answered the young angel, "and by suffering he will understand the meaning of all sorrow and pain; and he will be able to comfort everyone who cries; and his own tears will be for the healing of sad hearts; and those who are healed by him will learn for his sake to be kind to each other."

"But if the Son of God is a true man," said Uriel, "he must first be a child, simple, and lowly, and helpless. It may be that he will never gain the learning of the schools. The masters of earthly wisdom will despise him and speak scorn of him."

"I know it," said the young angel, "but in meekness will he answer them; and to those who become as little children he will give the heavenly wisdom that comes, without seeking, to the pure and gentle of heart."

"But if he becomes a man," said Michael, "evil men will hate and persecute him; they may even take his life, if they are stronger than he."

"I know it," answered the young angel. "They will nail him to a cross. But when he is lifted up he will draw all men unto him, for he will still be the Son of God, and no heart that is open to love can help loving him, since his love for men is so great that he is willing to die for them."

"But how do you know these things?" cried the other angels. "Who are you?"

"I am the Christmas angel," he said. "At first I was sent as the dream of a little child, a holy child, blessed and wonderful, to dwell in the heart of a pure virgin, Mary of Nazareth. There I was hidden till the word came to call me back to the throne of the King, and tell me my name, and give me my new message. For this is Christmas Day on Earth, and to-day the Son of God is born of a woman. So I must fly quickly, before the sun rises, to bring the good news to those happy men who have been chosen to receive them."

As he said this, the young angel rose, with arms outspread, from the green meadow of Peacefield and, passing over the bounds of Heaven, dropped swiftly as a shooting-star toward the night shadow of the Earth. The other angels followed him—a throng of dazzling forms, beautiful as a rain of jewels falling from the dark-blue sky. But the child-angel went more swifly than the others, because of the certainty of gladness in his heart.

And as the others followed him they wondered who had been favoured and chosen to receive the glad tidings.

"It must be the Emperor of the World and his counsellors," they thought. But the flight passed over Rome.

"It may be the philosophers and the master of learning," they thought. But the flight passed over Athens.

"Can it be the High Priest of the Jews, and the elders and the scribes?" they thought. But the flight passed over Jerusalem.

It floated out over the hill country of Bethlehem; the throng of silent angels holding close together, as if perplexed and doubtful; the child-angel darting on far in advance, as one who knew the way through the darkness.

The villages were all still: the very houses seemed asleep; but in one place there was a low sound of talking in a stable, near to an inn—a sound as of a mother soothing her baby to rest.

All over the pastures on the hillsides a light film of snow had fallen, delicate as the veil of a bride adorned for the marriage; and as the child-angel passed over them, alone in the swiftness of his flight, the pure fields sparkled round him, giving back his radiance.

And there were in that country shepherds abiding in the fields, keeping watch over their flocks by night. And lo! the angel of the Lord came upon them, and the glory of the Lord shone round about them, and they were sore afraid. And the angel said unto them: "Fear not; for behold I bring you glad tidings of great joy which shall be to all nations. For unto you is born this day, in the city of David, a Savior, which is Christ the Lord. And this shall be a sign unto you; ye shall find the babe wrapped in swaddling clothes, lying in a manger."

And suddenly there was with the angel a multitude of the heavenly host, praising God and saying: "Glory to God in the highest, and on earth peace, good-will toward men." And the shepherds said one to another: "Let us now go, even to Bethlehem, and see this thing which is come to pass."

So I said within myself that I also would go with the shepherds, even to Bethlehem. And I heard a great and sweet voice, as of a bell, which said, "Come!" And when the bell had sounded twelve times, I awoke; and it was Christmas morn; and I knew that I had been in a dream.

Yet it seemed to me that the things which I had heard were true.

A Prayer for
Christmas Morning

 he day of joy returns
Father in Heaven, and
crowns another year with peace
and good will.

Help us rightly to remember the birth of Jesus,
that we may share in the song of the angels, the
gladness of the shepherds, and the worship of the
wisemen.

Close the doors of hate and open the doors of
love all over the world. . . .

Let kindness come with every gift and good
desires with every greeting.

Deliver us from evil, by the blessing that Christ
brings, and teach us to be merry with clean hearts.

May the Christmas morning make us happy to
be thy children, and the Christmas evening bring us
to our bed with grateful thoughts, forgiving and
forgiven, for Jesus sake. Amen.